ARIZONA TEST PREP

Revising and Editing

Practice Workbook

Grade 3

ISBN 978-1726823722

TEST MASTER PRESS

www.testmasterpress.com

CONTENTS

INTRODUCTION
For Parents, Teachers, and Tutors

Developing Writing and Language Skills

Arizona's 2016 English Language Arts standards describe what students are expected to know. Student learning is based on these standards throughout the year, and the state tests cover these standards. All the questions in this book cover the skills listed in Arizona's 2016 English Language Arts standards.

This workbook focuses specifically on revising and editing skills. This covers the writing standard that describes how students need to be able to develop and strengthen writing by planning, revising, and editing. The editing questions cover the language standard describing how students demonstrate command of the conventions of standard English grammar, usage, capitalization, punctuation, and spelling, as well as the spelling skills listed in the Writing Foundational Skills. The questions also cover the language standards describing knowledge of language and vocabulary acquisition and use. In addition, the questions cover a range of writing skills necessary for producing writing of different types. These include remaining focused, developing a topic, linking ideas, expressing ideas clearly, writing varied sentences, and using words and phrases for effect.

Revising and Editing Practice

Each practice set in this book provides practice with both revising and editing tasks. Revising questions involve making changes to strengthen writing. This involve tasks like adding sentences, combining sentences, simplifying sentences, making stronger word choices, removing irrelevant information, and using effective transition words and phrases. Editing tasks involve making changes to correct errors. These errors cover grammar, usage, capitalization, punctuation, and spelling.

Completing the Practice Sets

Each practice set in this book contains an example of student writing that contains errors or opportunities for improvement. Each passage is followed by 18 multiple choice questions that ask students to identify and correct an error, or choose the best way to improve the passage. Student work can be checked after each practice set to determine progress and provide feedback. In this way, students can develop and improve their skills as they complete the sets.

Preparing for the AzMERIT English Language Arts Assessments

Students in Arizona take the AzMERIT English Language Arts assessments each year. The AzMERIT tests assess language skills by including editing tasks. Students complete these tasks by identifying and correcting errors in grammar, usage, capitalization, punctuation, and spelling. This workbook will prepare students for these questions.

The AzMERIT tests also include writing tasks. These tasks are scored for overall writing ability. The features expected of student writing include remaining focused, having an effective structure, expressing ideas clearly, using effective transitions, using language effectively, and using varied sentences. These tasks are also scored for writing conventions. The activities in this book will develop strong writing skills and improve student performance on these writing tasks.

Revising and Editing

Practice Sets

Instructions for Students

Read each passage. Each passage contains errors or opportunities for improvement. The questions following each passage will ask you how to correct an error or how to improve the passage.

The sentences in the passage are numbered. Each question will give the sentence number or the paragraph number the question is about. You can reread the sentence to help you answer the question, and some questions may require you to reread a paragraph to answer the question. You can look back at the passage as often as you like.

For each multiple choice question, read the question carefully. Then select the best answer. Fill in the circle for the correct answer.

Passage 1

Aubrey was asked to write a letter to a future babysitter. Aubrey wrote the letter that follows. Read the letter and look for any changes that should be made. Then answer the questions that follow.

Dear Babysitter

Dear Babysitter,

(1) I am writing to introduce you to my family. (2) My name is Aubrey. (3) I am nine years old and have two brothers who are both younger than me. (4) My brother, James, is seven, and my other brother, Colin, is two and a half. (5) We love having babysitters because we get to play games and watch movies with them. (6) I have some suggestions for you before you began babysitting.

(7) My first peace of advice is to watch Colin really carefully. (8) James and I love our baby brother, Colin, but he can be hard to keep track of. (9) Colin just learned how to run and he likes to run around the house all of the time. (10) Sometimes we distract Colin with his favorite toy, he is a dancing Elmo. (11) Colin loves to dance along with Elmo and clap his hands. (12) James and I like to play in the basement. (13) Colin can join us down there and play with his toys. (14) Sometimes James likes to play video games, I like to play with my iPad. (15) I can show you some of my favorite apps!

(16) For dinner, my parents give us a vegetable or fruit with a main dish. (17) Our main dish is usually chicken nuggets lasagne or soup. (18) Colin loves peanut butter and jelly sandwiches cut up into tiny pieces. (19) Colin cannot chew well.

(20) James, Colin, and I love to play games with our babysitters. (21) Our most favorite games are CandyLand, Chutes and Ladders, and Simon Says. (22) Colin isn't old enough to play these games but he likes to pretend he's playing with us. (23) We also like to watch movies. (24) Last week, we watch *Frozen* and *Zootopia*. (25) We can show you how to use the remotes so that we can watch movies together.

(26) Before bed, we all have a routine. (27) We all brush our tooths, get our pajamas on, and read one or two books. (28) You might also like to read a story to Colin because he can't read on his own yet. (29) Colin goes to bed around 7 o'clock and James and I go to bed a bit past that.

(30) We can't wait to meet you! (31) I think we're going to have lots of fun together.

Sincerely,

Aubrey Jackson

****

Aubrey Jackson
89 Parkway Drive Dallas Texas

1   The end of sentence 3 can be rewritten to express the ideas in a simpler way. Which of these shows the best way to rewrite the sentence?

Ⓐ   I am nine years old and have two brothers younger.

Ⓑ   I am nine years old and have two younger brothers.

Ⓒ   I am nine years old and younger brothers have two.

Ⓓ   I am nine years old and have younger brothers two.

2   Aubrey wants to rewrite sentence 4 to express the ideas in a simpler way. Which of these shows the best way to rewrite the sentence?

Ⓐ   James is seven, while Colin is two and a half.

Ⓑ   James and Colin, are seven and two and a half.

Ⓒ   My brothers are, James, seven, and Colin, two and a half.

Ⓓ   My brother named James is seven, my other brother named Colin is two and a half.

3   In sentence 6, which word should replace *began*?

Ⓐ   begin

Ⓑ   begins

Ⓒ   beginner

Ⓓ   beginning

4   Which change should be made in sentence 7?

    Ⓐ   Change *peace* to *piece*

    Ⓑ   Change *advice* to *advise*

    Ⓒ   Change *watch* to *watching*

    Ⓓ   Change *carefully* to *careful*

5   Aubrey wants to add a sentence to connect the ideas in sentences 9 and 10. Which sentence would Aubrey be best to add after sentence 9?

    Ⓐ   He has many toys, but Elmo is his favorite.

    Ⓑ   Colin goes to sports classes every Tuesday.

    Ⓒ   It is best if you can get him to sit still.

    Ⓓ   We often wonder how he has so much energy.

6   Sentence 10 does not use the correct words after the comma. Which of these shows the correct words to use?

    Ⓐ   Sometimes we distract Colin with his favorite toy, who is a dancing Elmo.

    Ⓑ   Sometimes we distract Colin with his favorite toy, that is a dancing Elmo.

    Ⓒ   Sometimes we distract Colin with his favorite toy, and is a dancing Elmo.

    Ⓓ   Sometimes we distract Colin with his favorite toy, which is a dancing Elmo.

7   In sentence 14, which word should be added after the comma?

Ⓐ   while

Ⓑ   then

Ⓒ   or

Ⓓ   and

8   Aubrey wants to add a sentence to introduce the ideas in paragraph 3. Which sentence would Aubrey be best to add before sentence 16?

Ⓐ   It is important to have healthy meals every day.

Ⓑ   If you stay for the evening, you will also need to give us all dinner.

Ⓒ   Looking after us all day might make you hungry.

Ⓓ   My parents look after us very well when they are home.

9   Which of these shows the correct way to place commas in sentence 17?

Ⓐ   Our main dish is usually, chicken nuggets lasagne or soup.

Ⓑ   Our main dish is usually, chicken nuggets, lasagne, or soup.

Ⓒ   Our main dish is usually chicken nuggets, lasagne, or soup.

Ⓓ   Our main dish is usually chicken nuggets, lasagne, or, soup.

10   Which of these shows the best way to combine sentences 18 and 19?

    Ⓐ   Colin loves peanut butter and jelly sandwiches cut up into tiny pieces, cannot chew well.

    Ⓑ   Colin loves peanut butter and jelly sandwiches cut up into tiny pieces, he cannot chew well.

    Ⓒ   Colin loves peanut butter and jelly sandwiches cut up into tiny pieces because cannot chew well.

    Ⓓ   Colin loves peanut butter and jelly sandwiches cut up into tiny pieces because he cannot chew well.

11   Which change should be made in sentence 21?

    Ⓐ   Delete the word *most*

    Ⓑ   Replace *favorite* with *favoring*

    Ⓒ   Replace *games* with *game's*

    Ⓓ   Delete the commas in the sentence

12   In sentence 22, what is *he's* short for?

    Ⓐ   he is

    Ⓑ   he was

    Ⓒ   he does

    Ⓓ   he plays

13   In sentence 24, which word should replace *watch*?

  Ⓐ watches

  Ⓑ watched

  Ⓒ watcher

  Ⓓ watching

14   Which change should be made in sentence 27?

  Ⓐ Replace *all* with *altogether*

  Ⓑ Replace *tooths* with *teeth*

  Ⓒ Replace *pajamas* with *pajama's*

  Ⓓ Replace *two* with *too*

15   The end of sentence 29 can be written more simply. Which of these shows the correct way to end sentence 29?

  Ⓐ Colin goes to bed around 7 o'clock and James and I go to bed a bit late.

  Ⓑ Colin goes to bed around 7 o'clock and James and I go to bed a bit later.

  Ⓒ Colin goes to bed around 7 o'clock and James and I go to bed a bit latest.

  Ⓓ Colin goes to bed around 7 o'clock and James and I go to bed a bit lateness.

16   Aubrey wants to add the sentence below to paragraph 5.

> After we are all asleep, my mom would love it if you cleaned up a little.

Where is the best place to add the sentence?

Ⓐ   After sentence 26

Ⓑ   After sentence 27

Ⓒ   After sentence 28

Ⓓ   After sentence 29

17   In sentence 31, which of these shows a phrase that could replace *lots* to express the idea in a more interesting way?

Ⓐ   I think we're going to have bits and pieces of fun together.

Ⓑ   I think we're going to have loads and loads of fun together.

Ⓒ   I think we're going to have better and better of fun together.

Ⓓ   I think we're going to have more or less of fun together.

18   Which of these shows the correct way to place commas in the address at the end of the passage?

Ⓐ   89 Parkway Drive, Dallas Texas

Ⓑ   89 Parkway Drive, Dallas, Texas

Ⓒ   89, Parkway Drive, Dallas Texas

Ⓓ   89, Parkway Drive, Dallas, Texas

END OF PRACTICE SET

Passage 2

Larry was asked to write an essay about what he wants to be when he grows up. Larry wrote an essay about wanting to be a chef. Read the essay and look for any changes that should be made. Then answer the questions that follow.

I Want to Be A Chef!

 (1) When I grow up, I want to be a top chef! (2) I know I can be the best chef in the hole world if I really put my mind to it. (3) I want to open my own restaurant. (4) My grandfather makes the best food and he is my teacher. (5) I think that if I practice I can be the best.

(6) My grandfather owns the Starlite Diner in town. (7) I stay with him after I finish school at the diner sometimes. (8) He has teach me how to make spaghetti, scrambled eggs, pancakes, tacos, sandwiches, and hotdogs. (9) I want to learn to make diffrent foods from all over the world.

(10) When people come to the restaurant, I give them menus. (11) I show them wear to sit too. (12) My grandfather lets me bring them they drinks. (13) I want to be like my grandfather. (14) He is a great chef. (15) I also watch cooking shows on TV. (16) I like to watch *Top Chef*, and other cooking shows. (17) I see how chefs can make unique foods from stranje things. (18) I think I can make anything if I try. (19) I watched one man make a lemon meringue pie and it looked delicious. (20) I want to cook and bake desserts.

(21) When I get older I want to go to school to become a professional chef. (22) Mom want me to go to school so I can become the best chef in the world. (23) She says I can be a great chef like my grandfather, I don't know if I can be that good.

(24) I know I can become a great chef because I am practicing every day. (25) I also learn how to cook at home with Mom. (26) She has showed me how to make many things. (27) Her family is from a small village in italy. (28) She is great at cooking Italian food. (29) She makes perfect lasagne, risotto, and, ravioli. (30) I help Mom with the garlic bread we make for dinner. (31) I can't tell you how we make it because it's a secret recipe! (32) My grandfather often let me make garlic bread at the diner too. (33) I know I can be on *Top Chef* someday!

(34) When I am older, I will impress everyone with my cooking! (35) I might have to work in other people's restaurants at first. (36) That's okay because I will use that time to study as much I can. (37) I will soak in everything I see, just like I have in my grandfather's diner. (38) Then finally, I will open my own restaurant. (39) I would love to name it George's after my amazing grandfather. (40) That is what I dream of, and one day I will make it happen.

I will make wonderful dishes that will not be forgotten!

1   Which word capitalized in the title should be in lower case?

    Ⓐ   Want

    Ⓑ   Be

    Ⓒ   A

    Ⓓ   Chef

2   Which change should be made in sentence 2?

    Ⓐ   Change *know* to *no*

    Ⓑ   Change *be* to *bee*

    Ⓒ   Change *hole* to *whole*

    Ⓓ   Change *mind* to *mined*

3   Which of these shows the correct place for a comma in sentence 5?

    Ⓐ   I think, that if I practice I can be the best.

    Ⓑ   I think that if, I practice I can be the best.

    Ⓒ   I think that if I practice, I can be the best.

    Ⓓ   I think that if I practice I can be, the best.

4   Sentence 7 can be written more clearly. Which of these is the best way to rewrite sentence 7?

    Ⓐ   I sometimes stay with him after I finish school at the diner.

    Ⓑ   I sometimes stay with him at the diner after I finish school.

    Ⓒ   I stay with him sometimes at the diner after I finish school.

    Ⓓ   I stay with him sometimes after I finish school at the diner.

5   Which word should replace *teach* in sentence 8?

    Ⓐ   taught

    Ⓑ   teaches

    Ⓒ   teached

    Ⓓ   teaching

6   In sentence 9, what is the correct way to spell *diffrent*?

    Ⓐ   difirent

    Ⓑ   diferent

    Ⓒ   different

    Ⓓ   diffirent

7   What is the correct way to write sentence 11?

(A)   I show them we're to sit to.

(B)   I show them we're to sit too.

(C)   I show them where to sit to.

(D)   I show them where to sit too.

8   Which of these shows the word that should replace *they* in sentence 12?

(A)   My grandfather lets me bring them they'll drinks.

(B)   My grandfather lets me bring them their drinks.

(C)   My grandfather lets me bring them there drinks.

(D)   My grandfather lets me bring them they're drinks.

9   Which change should be made in sentence 17?

(A)   Change *chefs* to *chef's*

(B)   Change *make* to *made*

(C)   Change *from* to *for*

(D)   Change *stranje* to *strange*

10   Which word or phrase should replace *want* in sentence 22?

Ⓐ   wants

Ⓑ   wanting

Ⓒ   did want

Ⓓ   does want

11   In sentence 23, which word should be added after the comma?

Ⓐ   and

Ⓑ   but

Ⓒ   or

Ⓓ   for

12   Which of these shows sentence 27 with the correct capitalization?

Ⓐ   Her Family is from a small village in italy.

Ⓑ   Her family is from a small village in Italy.

Ⓒ   Her Family is from a small village in Italy.

Ⓓ   Her family is from a small Village in Italy.

13   Which of these shows the correct way to punctuate sentence 29?

    Ⓐ   She makes perfect, lasagne risotto and ravioli.

    Ⓑ   She makes perfect lasagne risotto, and, ravioli.

    Ⓒ   She makes perfect lasagne, risotto, and ravioli.

    Ⓓ   She makes perfect, lasagne, risotto, and ravioli.

14   In sentence 31, what is *it's* short for?

    Ⓐ   it is

    Ⓑ   it has

    Ⓒ   it was

    Ⓓ   it does

15   Which change should be made in sentence 32?

    Ⓐ   Change *often* to *offen*

    Ⓑ   Change *let* to *lets*

    Ⓒ   Change *me* to *mine*

    Ⓓ   Change *make* to *made*

16   In sentence 37, what does the phrase "soak in" refer to?

    Ⓐ   baking

    Ⓑ   cleaning

    Ⓒ   learning

    Ⓓ   resting

17   In sentence 38, Larry wants to replace *finally* with a different word. Which of these shows a word that makes sense in the sentence?

    Ⓐ   Then someday, I will open my own restaurant.

    Ⓑ   Then someone, I will open my own restaurant.

    Ⓒ   Then somewhere, I will open my own restaurant.

    Ⓓ   Then something, I will open my own restaurant.

18   Which of these shows a correct way to rewrite the caption at the end of the passage?

    Ⓐ   I will make wonderful dishes that will be forgetful!

    Ⓑ   I will make wonderful dishes that will be forgettable!

    Ⓒ   I will make wonderful dishes that will be unforgettable!

    Ⓓ   I will make wonderful dishes that will be forgot!

END OF PRACTICE SET

Passage 3

The students in Pashk's class were asked to write a biography about an important person. Pashk wrote a biography about Mother Teresa. Read the biography and look for any changes that should be made. Then answer the questions that follow.

Mother Teresa

(1) Mother Teresa was a well-loved humanitarian of the 20th century. (2) She was born in Albania on August 25 1910. (3) She died on September 5, 1997. (4) Mother Teresa served the poor in India and in other Countries. (5) She is honored by many people and the Catholic Church for her service to the poor. (6) She recieved the Nobel Peace Prize for her work in 1979 and became a saint in 2016.

(7) Mother Teresa is born with the name Agnes Bojaxhiu. (8) Her mother taught her to always feed the poor when she was a child. (9) She went to an elementary school run by nuns. (10) Mother Teresa went on a pilgrimage when she was 12. (11) She wanted become a nun. (12) At 18, she joined the Sisters of Loreto in Dublin, Ireland. (13) Later she went with the sisters to India. (14) She worked at a high school for poor girls in India. (15) She taught history and she taught geography too. (16) She also learned Hindi and Bengali in India. (17) She made final vows to the Sisters of Loreto in 1937. (18) She changed her name to Mother Teresa when she made final vows. (19) In 1946, she want to leave the nuns to work with the poor every day. (20) In 1948, the Pope gave her permission to leave the sisters.

(21) She was determined to give poor people the opportunity to learn. (22) She believed that this was the way for people to overcome poverty. (23) She went to live in the poorest areas of India where she believed that people needed her the most. (24) First, she opened an open-air school for poor students. (25) When people saw the work that she was doing, they helped her. (26) People gave money and time to helping her. (27) Mother Teresa opened an orphanage, a nurseing home, and many clinics in India. (28) She got many people to volunteer with her.

(29) In 1971, she went to America. (30) She opened a home for poor people in America. (31) She also went to Beirut and Armenia to help people. (32) Mother Teresa died in 1997 because of heart lung and kidney problems. (33) She win many awards for the good things she did. (34) Mother Teresa is thought of by many people as the most great saint of all time. (35) She gave to others without thought for herself.

© Zvonimir Atletic / Shutterstock.com

A statue in India honors the great work she did.

1   Which of these shows the correct way to punctuate the date in sentence 2?

Ⓐ   She was born in Albania on August, 25 1910.

Ⓑ   She was born in Albania on August 25, 1910.

Ⓒ   She was born in Albania on August, 25, 1910.

Ⓓ   She was born in Albania on, August 25 1910.

2   Which word in the first paragraph should NOT be capitalized?

Ⓐ   Albania

Ⓑ   September

Ⓒ   India

Ⓓ   Countries

3   Which change should be made in sentence 6?

Ⓐ   Change *recieved* to *received*

Ⓑ   Change *Nobel Peace Prize* to *Nobel peace prize*

Ⓒ   Change *her* to *their*

Ⓓ   Change *became* to *become*

4   Which word should replace *is* in sentence 7?

    Ⓐ   are

    Ⓑ   did

    Ⓒ   was

    Ⓓ   were

5   Sentence 8 can be rewritten to make the meaning clearer. What is the best way to rewrite sentence 8?

    Ⓐ   Her mother taught her when she was a child to always feed the poor.

    Ⓑ   To always feed the poor, her mother taught her when she was a child.

    Ⓒ   When she was a child, her mother taught her to always feed the poor.

    Ⓓ   When she was a child, to always feed the poor, her mother taught her.

6   In sentence 11, which of these has the correct word added after *wanted* to form a complete sentence?

    Ⓐ   She wanted so become a nun.

    Ⓑ   She wanted to become a nun.

    Ⓒ   She wanted and become a nun.

    Ⓓ   She wanted then become a nun.

7   Which of these shows the correct way to write sentence 13?

Ⓐ   Later, she went with the sisters to India.

Ⓑ   Later she went, with the sisters to India.

Ⓒ   Later she went with, the sisters to India.

Ⓓ   Later she went with the sisters, to India.

8   Which of these is the best way to write sentence 15 more simply?

Ⓐ   She taught history and taught geography.

Ⓑ   She taught history, taught geography too.

Ⓒ   She taught history and geography.

Ⓓ   She taught history, geography too.

9   In sentence 19, which word should replace *want*?

Ⓐ   wants

Ⓑ   wanted

Ⓒ   wanting

Ⓓ   wanter

10   Pashk wants to add a topic sentence to paragraph 3. Which of these would be the best sentence to add to the start of the paragraph?

    Ⓐ   Showing kindness is one simple way that everyone can help others.

    Ⓑ   Being a volunteer is very worthwhile.

    Ⓒ   Mother Teresa helped many people, and inspired others to help as well.

    Ⓓ   Mother Teresa was not paid for the work she did.

11   In sentence 21, what does the word *opportunity* mean?

    Ⓐ   chance

    Ⓑ   decision

    Ⓒ   hope

    Ⓓ   motivation

12   Which word should replace *helping* in sentence 26?

    Ⓐ   help

    Ⓑ   helps

    Ⓒ   helped

    Ⓓ   helpful

13 In sentence 27, what is the correct way to spell *nurseing*?

Ⓐ nursing

Ⓑ nurssing

Ⓒ nerseing

Ⓓ nersing

14 Which of these is the best way to combine sentences 29 and 30?

Ⓐ In 1971, she went to America, opened a home for poor people in America.

Ⓑ In 1971, she went to America, opened a home for poor people.

Ⓒ In 1971, she went to America and opened a home for poor people in America.

Ⓓ In 1971, she went to America and opened a home for poor people.

15 Which of these shows the correct use of commas in sentence 32?

Ⓐ Mother Teresa died in 1997 because of, heart lung and kidney problems.

Ⓑ Mother Teresa died in 1997 because of heart, lung, and kidney problems.

Ⓒ Mother Teresa died in 1997 because of heart, lung, and kidney, problems.

Ⓓ Mother Teresa died in 1997 because of heart lung, and kidney problems.

16   Which of these shows the correct way to write sentence 33?

Ⓐ   She win many award for the good things she did.

Ⓑ   She win many award's for the good things she did.

Ⓒ   She won many awards for the good things she did.

Ⓓ   She won many award for the good things she did.

17   In sentence 34, which word should replace "most great"?

Ⓐ   greater

Ⓑ   greatly

Ⓒ   greatest

Ⓓ   greatness

18   Pashk wants to add a final sentence to end the passage. Which sentence would Pashk be best to add after sentence 35?

Ⓐ   Everyone can make a difference if they try.

Ⓑ   The loss of Mother Teresa was a sad day.

Ⓒ   Her kindness and generosity will never be forgotten.

Ⓓ   She died in Calcutta, India, and received a state funeral.

END OF PRACTICE SET

Passage 4

Elizabeth's teacher asked the class to write a story about a family trip. Elizabeth wrote about her weekend at the beach with her family. Read the story and look for any changes that should be made. Then answer the questions that follow.

having fun at the beach

(1) Last summer, my whole family traveled to california to visit the beach. (2) My mom, dad, little brother, little sister and me drove for a long time. (3) We were in the car for three and a half hours. (4) When we got to the beach, Dad said we have to go to the hotel first. (5) I got angry because I wanted to see the ocean. (6) Dad left us in the car with Mom and told us to wait. (7) When he came back, he had a key to our hotel room. (8) I was excited about staying in a hotel. (9) I forgot all about being angry.

(10) I took my backpack and my stuffed lion from the car. (11) Next I climbed the stairs all the way to the top floor. (12) By the time I finally reeched the top floor, my legs were aching and wobbling a little bit! (13) After we unpacked, I asked Dad again to see the ocean. (14) He said I had to ask Mom. (15) I asked Mom and she said we would all go see the ocean together now. (16) Dad stayed in the hotel room and watched TV, he was tired from the drive.

(17) My brother, Marco, my sister, Ann, and Mom and I all walked to the beach. (18) I took my sandals off right away. (19) I loved the feeling of the sand under my toes. (20) I couldn't beleeve sand could be so soft.

(21) I am so excited when we picked a place to sit. (22) Mom dug a hole and put an umbrella in the sand. (23) Then we all ran to the ocean. (24) Mom got scared because Marco is only 4 years old and he ran straight into the ocean. (25) I stayed right by Marcos side to make sure he would be safe. (26) He was laughing the whole time, and had a blast!

(27) I splashed Ann with water and she laughed too. (28) We wanted to build a sand castle. (29) Ann and I take turn filling the bucket with water and building the castle. (30) We made a huge castle with lots of shells pressed into the side for decorate. (31) Dad came down to the beach and took a picture of the sand castle. (32) We all walked down the beach together, and Dad found a really nice shell. (33) He taught me a new word. (34) Shell called a conch shell. (35) I did not want to lose the shell, so I put it in my pocket.

(36) I loved the beach so much! (37) We stayed one night and two days at the beach only. (38) My parents said we will go back again next year. (39) I hope we can go again more soon. (40) I had so much fun and I will never forget the trip! (41) I still have my conch shell too! (42) Conch shells are large shells that were once home to sea snails. (43) I keep my shell on my bookshelf next to the photograph that my dad took.

1   Which of these is the correct way to capitalize the title?

Ⓐ   Having fun at the Beach

Ⓑ   Having Fun at the Beach

Ⓒ   Having Fun at The Beach

Ⓓ   Having Fun At The Beach

2   Which word in the first sentence should be capitalized?

Ⓐ   summer

Ⓑ   family

Ⓒ   california

Ⓓ   beach

3   In sentence 2, which word should replace *me*?

Ⓐ   I

Ⓑ   we

Ⓒ   us

Ⓓ   them

4   In sentence 4, which words should replace "have to go"?

    Ⓐ   had to go

    Ⓑ   had to gone

    Ⓒ   have to gone

    Ⓓ   have to went

5   Which of these is the best way to combine sentences 8 and 9?

    Ⓐ   I was excited about staying in a hotel, so I forgot all about being angry.

    Ⓑ   I was excited about staying in a hotel, yet I forgot all about being angry.

    Ⓒ   I was excited about staying in a hotel, but I forgot all about being angry.

    Ⓓ   I was excited about staying in a hotel, or I forgot all about being angry.

6   Which word in sentence 12 is spelled incorrectly?

    Ⓐ   finally

    Ⓑ   reeched

    Ⓒ   aching

    Ⓓ   wobbling

7   Sentence 16 needs the comma to be replaced with a word that connects the two ideas. Which of these shows the correct way to write sentence 16?

Ⓐ   Dad stayed in the hotel room and watched TV although he was tired from the drive.

Ⓑ   Dad stayed in the hotel room and watched TV also he was tired from the drive.

Ⓒ   Dad stayed in the hotel room and watched TV because he was tired from the drive.

Ⓓ   Dad stayed in the hotel room and watched TV however he was tired from the drive.

8   Which change should be made in sentence 20?

Ⓐ   Change *couldn't* to *could'nt*

Ⓑ   Change *beleeve* to *believe*

Ⓒ   Change *be* to *bee*

Ⓓ   Change *soft* to *softly*

9   In sentence 21, which word should replace *am*?

Ⓐ   is

Ⓑ   are

Ⓒ   was

Ⓓ   were

10   Which change should be made in sentence 25?

   Ⓐ   Change *right* to *write*

   Ⓑ   Change *Marco* to *Marco's*

   Ⓒ   Change *sure* to *shore*

   Ⓓ   Change *be* to *being*

11   As it is used in sentence 26, what does the phrase "had a blast" tell you about Marco?

   Ⓐ   Marco made a lot of noise.

   Ⓑ   Marco had a very good time.

   Ⓒ   Marco hurt himself.

   Ⓓ   Marco got in trouble.

12   In sentence 29, which words should replace "take turn"?

   Ⓐ   take turns

   Ⓑ   took turn

   Ⓒ   took turns

   Ⓓ   taking turn

13   In sentence 30, *decorate* is not the right word to end the sentence with. Which of these shows the correct word?

    Ⓐ   We made a huge castle with lots of shells pressed into the side for decorated.

    Ⓑ   We made a huge castle with lots of shells pressed into the side for decorator.

    Ⓒ   We made a huge castle with lots of shells pressed into the side for decorative.

    Ⓓ   We made a huge castle with lots of shells pressed into the side for decoration.

14   Which sentence in paragraph 5 is NOT a complete sentence?

    Ⓐ   Sentence 31

    Ⓑ   Sentence 32

    Ⓒ   Sentence 33

    Ⓓ   Sentence 34

15   In sentence 35, what is the correct way to shorten "did not"?

    Ⓐ   do'nt

    Ⓑ   don't

    Ⓒ   did'nt

    Ⓓ   didn't

16   Sentence 37 can be improved by moving the word *only*. Which of these is the best way to rewrite the sentence?

Ⓐ   We only stayed one night and two days at the beach.

Ⓑ   We stayed one night only and two days at the beach.

Ⓒ   We stayed one night and two days only at the beach.

Ⓓ   We stayed one night and two days at the only beach.

17   In sentence 39, which word or phrase should replace "more soon"?

Ⓐ   sooner

Ⓑ   soonest

Ⓒ   more sooner

Ⓓ   more soonest

18   Elizabeth wants to remove a sentence that does not fit well in the last paragraph. Which sentence would Elizabeth be best to remove?

Ⓐ   Sentence 40

Ⓑ   Sentence 41

Ⓒ   Sentence 42

Ⓓ   Sentence 43

END OF PRACTICE SET

Passage 5

Rose's teacher asked the students to write a persuasive letter about a school rule. Rose asked the principal to remove the rule about school uniforms. Read the letter and look for any changes that should be made. Then answer the questions that follow.

I Don't Want to Wear a Uniform

Dear principal carlita sanchez

(1) I think that we should not wear uniforms. (2) Every day we have to wear the same clothing, it is boring. (3) School uniforms make us all look the same. (4) I do not want to wear the same thing every day because I want to wear my own clothes. (5) My clothes make me feel good about me. (6) I also know my friends want to wear there favorite shirts and jeans. (7) I know that the uniform makes us all look the same, but I don't think it helps us. (8) We want to express ourselves through our clothing.

(9) I promise that I won't wear clothing with bad words or holes. (10) I just want to wear things that I like. (11) You can still made rules about what we can wear, but we don't like the uniforms. (12) My friends and I want to wear t-shirts, jeans, and hoodies, and even dresses or skirts to school. (13) We also want to be allowed to wear shorts in the warmer whether.

(14) I want to wear clothing that is comforttable so I can focus in school. (15) I also don't like the uniform because it is itch. (16) I hate to wear the wool skirt in the winter, and it always slides around my stomach. (17) In the winter, I want to wear jeans, because my legs are cold when I walk to school. (18) The other girls in my class agree me. (19) They don't like the skirt either.

(20) I talked to the boys also. (21) They said they don't like their shirts or their pants. (22) The boys said they do not like the school rule about uniforms. (23) Both the girls and boys at our school want to wear their own clothing. (24) If we wear our clothing we won't say bad things anymore about the uniform.

(25) My mom also says that the uniforms are external and she cannot afford to buy me another skirt. (26) I have to wear the same skirt all week and wash it every evening. (27) My mom gets mad at me when I spill my lemonade on my skirt or shirt. (28) I can save my mom money if I don't have to wear a uniform no more.

(29) Eventually, I think all the students will be happy if there is no rule about uniforms. (30) We can write new rules about a dress code and you can read them and agree to them. (31) We just want to be comfortable and warm. (32) We also want to wear our favorite things and feel good about us.

(33) Thank you for your time.

Sincerely

Rose Camille

We get tired of wearing the same thing every day!

1   Which of these is the correct way to write the opening of the letter?

    Ⓐ   Dear principal Carlita Sanchez.

    Ⓑ   Dear principal Carlita Sanchez,

    Ⓒ   Dear Principal Carlita Sanchez.

    Ⓓ   Dear Principal Carlita Sanchez,

2   In sentence 2, which word should be added after the comma?

    Ⓐ   and

    Ⓑ   then

    Ⓒ   when

    Ⓓ   for

3   In sentence 5, which word should replace *me*?

    Ⓐ   I

    Ⓑ   mine

    Ⓒ   myself

    Ⓓ   ourself

4   Which change should be made in sentence 6?

Ⓐ   Change *know* to *no*

Ⓑ   Change *wear* to *where*

Ⓒ   Change *there* to *their*

Ⓓ   Change *jeans* to *genes*

5   In sentence 9, what is the word *won't* short for?

Ⓐ   was not

Ⓑ   will not

Ⓒ   were not

Ⓓ   would not

6   In sentence 11, which of these should replace *made*?

Ⓐ   make

Ⓑ   making

Ⓒ   have make

Ⓓ   been made

7   Which change should be made in sentence 13?

Ⓐ   Change *allowed* to *allowwed*

Ⓑ   Change *shorts* to *short's*

Ⓒ   Change *warmer* to *warmly*

Ⓓ   Change *whether* to *weather*

8   In sentence 14, what is the correct way to spell *comforttable*?

Ⓐ   comfforttable

Ⓑ   comffortabel

Ⓒ   comfortable

Ⓓ   comfortabel

9   In sentence 15, which word should replace *itch*?

Ⓐ   itches

Ⓑ   itchy

Ⓒ   itchful

Ⓓ   itchiness

10   Which of these adds the correct word to make sentence 18 a complete
      sentence?

      Ⓐ   The other girls in my class agree at me.

      Ⓑ   The other girls in my class agree to me.

      Ⓒ   The other girls in my class agree for me.

      Ⓓ   The other girls in my class agree with me.

11   Sentence 20 can be rearranged to sound better. Which of these places the word
      also in the best spot?

      Ⓐ   I also talked to the boys.

      Ⓑ   I talked also to the boys.

      Ⓒ   I talked to also the boys.

      Ⓓ   I talked to the also boys.

12   The word *external* is not the right word for sentence 25. Which word should
      replace *external*?

      Ⓐ   excellent

      Ⓑ   examined

      Ⓒ   expensive

      Ⓓ   explored

13   Which of these shows the correct way to end sentence 28?

Ⓐ   I can save my mom money if I don't have to wear a uniform never.

Ⓑ   I can save my mom money if I don't have to wear a uniform nothing.

Ⓒ   I can save my mom money if I don't have to wear a uniform sometime.

Ⓓ   I can save my mom money if I don't have to wear a uniform anymore.

14   At the start of sentence 29, which of these would be a better transition word than *eventually*?

Ⓐ   however

Ⓑ   although

Ⓒ   overall

Ⓓ   similarly

15   In sentence 32, *us* is not the correct word to use. Which of these shows the correct word to use?

Ⓐ   We also want to wear our favorite things and feel good about myself.

Ⓑ   We also want to wear our favorite things and feel good about ourselves.

Ⓒ   We also want to wear our favorite things and feel good about themselves.

Ⓓ   We also want to wear our favorite things and feel good about oneself.

16   Which sentence could best be added after sentence 32 to complete the paragraph?

Ⓐ   Taking away the rules about wearing uniforms will be great for everyone, and I hope you will consider it.

Ⓑ   Students will probably make smart choices about what to wear even if there are no rules.

Ⓒ   Many adults wear uniforms as part of their jobs.

Ⓓ   The weather changes throughout the year, and so will our clothing.

17   Which of these is the correct way to write the closing greeting of the letter?

Ⓐ   Sincerely!

Ⓑ   Sincerely,

Ⓒ   Sincerely?

Ⓓ   Sincerely.

18   Rose wants to add a word to the caption to emphasize how boring wearing the same thing all the time is. Which of these shows the best word to add?

Ⓐ   We get tired of wearing the same thing every silly day!

Ⓑ   We get tired of wearing the same thing every school day!

Ⓒ   We get tired of wearing the same thing every single day!

Ⓓ   We get tired of wearing the same thing every summer day!

END OF PRACTICE SET

Passage 6

Ethan was asked to write a biography for history class. He wrote the following biography about Walt Disney. Read the biography and look for any changes that should be made. Then answer the questions that follow.

The Life of Walt Disney

(1) Walt Disney was Born in Chicago on December the 5th, 1901. (2) He had four brother and one sister. (3) As a child, Walt loved drawing and cartooning. (4) He often contributed his work to the school newspaper. (5) He also sold his artwork to neighbors for extra money.

(6) When he leave school, Walt wanted to be a newspaper artist and cartoonist. (7) Walts brother Roy managed to get Walt a job in an art studio. (8) There he met Ub Iwerks, a talented and respected cartoonist. (9) Meeting Ub would inspire Walt to continue with his art and to continue with his drawing.

(10) Walt wanted to combine his love of drawing and his newfound love of animation. (11) He opened his own animation business. (12) Walt and his friend Fred Harman began creating cartoons they called 'Laugh-O-Grams.'

(13) Walt was then able to buy his own big studio. (14) He employing many people and began creating seven minute animations based on certain fairy tales. (15) Sadder, in 1923, he was forced to close the studio.

(16) Walt moved with his brother Roy to Hollywood. (17) With Roy and his friend Ub Iwerks, Walt started a new company called Disney Brothers' Studio. (18) They began creating new characters. (19) One of there finest creations was Mickey Mouse. (20) They produced an animation featuring motion pictures and sound called *Steamboat Willie*. (21) This cartoon was a huge hit.

(22) In 1929, they created new characters such as Minnie Mouse, Donald Duck, Goofy, and Pluto. (23) Them characters appeared in many new cartoons. (24) In 1937, they also produced the first full-length animated film called *Snow White and the Seven Dwarfs*. (25) It was very successful and they win many awards for this film.

(26) Walt and Walt's team would go on to make many more animated films. (27) After 1950, he began working on famous works such as *Cinderella*, *Alice in Wonderland*, *Peter Pan*, *Sleeping Beauty*, and *101 Dalmatians*. (28) In 1964, he produced *Mary Poppins*, which combined live action and animation.

(29) Walt's characters was the inspiration behind the first Disneyland in California. (30) Disneyland was a theme park for child and their families. (31) Visitors could meet Disney's characters and enjoy rides there too. (32) Even today, there are many Disneyland theme parks around the world.

(33) Walt Disney died in 1966. (34) His achievements during his lifetime were truly amazeing. (35) He produced some of the most watched and loved characters and animated films. (36) He dreamed big, believed in himself, and achieved many things that seemed not possible.

1   Which word in sentence 1 should NOT be capitalized?

Ⓐ   Disney

Ⓑ   Born

Ⓒ   Chicago

Ⓓ   December

2   Which of these shows the correct way to use plurals in sentence 2?

Ⓐ   He had four brothers and one sister.

Ⓑ   He had four brother and one sisters.

Ⓒ   He had four brothers and one sisters.

Ⓓ   He had four brother and one sister.

3   In sentence 6, which word should replace *leave*?

Ⓐ   leaves

Ⓑ   left

Ⓒ   leaving

Ⓓ   leaved

4   Which change should be made in sentence 7?

Ⓐ   Change *Walts* to *Walt's*

Ⓑ   Change *managed* to *managged*

Ⓒ   Change *get* to *got*

Ⓓ   Change *an* to *a*

5   Which of these shows the best way to simplify sentence 9 without changing its meaning?

Ⓐ   Meeting Ub would inspire Walt to continue.

Ⓑ   Meeting Ub would inspire Walt to continue with his art and drawing.

Ⓒ   Meeting Ub would inspire Walt with his art and with his drawing.

Ⓓ   Meeting Ub would inspire Walt with art and drawing.

6   In sentence 10, which word should replace *and*?

Ⓐ   all

Ⓑ   but

Ⓒ   to

Ⓓ   with

7   In sentence 14, which word should replace *employing*?

    Ⓐ   employ

    Ⓑ   employs

    Ⓒ   employed

    Ⓓ   employer

8   In sentence 15, which word should replace *Sadder*?

    Ⓐ   Sad

    Ⓑ   Sadly

    Ⓒ   Sadden

    Ⓓ   Saddest

9   Which of these shows sentence 19 written correctly?

    Ⓐ   One of their finest creations was Mickey Mouse.

    Ⓑ   One of they're finest creations was Mickey Mouse.

    Ⓒ   Won of their finest creations was Mickey Mouse.

    Ⓓ   Won of they're finest creations was Mickey Mouse.

10   In sentence 21, the phrase "a huge hit" means that the cartoon was –

Ⓐ   costly

Ⓑ   funny

Ⓒ   popular

Ⓓ   shocking

11   In sentence 23, which word should replace *Them*?

Ⓐ   These

Ⓑ   This

Ⓒ   Whose

Ⓓ   Which

12   Which of these uses the correct verb tense to replace the word *win* in sentence 25?

Ⓐ   It was very successful and they won many awards for this film.

Ⓑ   It was very successful and they wins many awards for this film.

Ⓒ   It was very successful and they had won many awards for this film.

Ⓓ   It was very successful and they have win many awards for this film.

13   Which of these should replace *Walt's* in sentence 26?

    Ⓐ   it

    Ⓑ   his

    Ⓒ   him

    Ⓓ   them

14   Which change should be made in sentence 29?

    Ⓐ   Change *characters* to *character's*

    Ⓑ   Change *was* to *were*

    Ⓒ   Change *behind* to *become*

    Ⓓ   Change *first* to *ferst*

15   In sentence 30, which word should replace *child*?

    Ⓐ   childs

    Ⓑ   childish

    Ⓒ   children

    Ⓓ   childhood

16   Which sentence would best be added after sentence 31?

   Ⓐ   Disney World later opened in Florida.

   Ⓑ   The Walt Disney Company still makes movies today.

   Ⓒ   Walt Disney should have focused more on his movies.

   Ⓓ   Walt Disney received 26 Academy Awards.

17   Which word in sentence 34 is spelled incorrectly?

   Ⓐ   achievements

   Ⓑ   lifetime

   Ⓒ   truly

   Ⓓ   amazeing

18   In sentence 36, which of these should replace "not possible"?

   Ⓐ   inpossible

   Ⓑ   unpossible

   Ⓒ   impossible

   Ⓓ   dispossible

END OF PRACTICE SET

Passage 7

Erin wrote this essay about drawing. Read the essay and look for any changes that should be made. Then answer the questions that follow.

My Favorite Hobby: Drawing

(1) Everyone has different thing they like to do in their free time. (2) I like to draw. (3) I haven't take any drawing classes besides school art classes. (4) I just draw on my own. (5) I guess you could say that I learn by doing.

(6) Sometimes I look at books and find pictures to copy. (7) I like drawing animals, especially zoo animals. (8) I also like to draw different nature settings. (9) Because I love to be outdoors, I draw trees and flowers. (10) I draw the sky and the clouds, too. (11) At night, I draw the stars and constellations.

(12) Drawing is a fun hobby. (13) I don't need many supplies. (14) It does not cost much either. (15) I have, in my bedroom, a special desk for my drawing supplies. (16) I have drawing pads, charcoal pencils, colored pencils, and some mini dry erasers.

(17) I take a drawing pad to school every day. (18) In my free time at school, I draw. (19) And sometimes for our school projects, we can add drawings. (20) I like that. (21) My art teacher, which name is Miss Jones, knows that I love to draw. (22) She gave me information about the art club.

(23) The members of the art club meet every friday afternoon after school. (24) Once there was a children's illustrator who come. (25) She showed us some of her drawings. (26) Then she had us draw a picture. (27) I drew a giraffe that was tall with its baby giraffe.

Drawing is a lot of fun and an enjoyable way to pass the time. It is also a great way to relax.

(28) There are some other reason why I like drawing. (29) I like to be creative. (30) I can draw almost anywhere I go. (31) I can make my drawings useful. (32) After all, I make my own birthday cards for my family and friends. (33) I often give drawings to mine grandmother, too. (34) They always bright her day and make her smile.

(35) My hobby keeps me busy in my free time. (36) I feel very calm when I am drawing. (37) I like to see other people enjoy my drawings, too. (38) If you ask me, I think I will be drawing my whole life! (39) Who knows where drawing could take me. (40) I might even be an art teacher like Miss Jones or a fammos children's illustrator some day!

People love it when I give them birthday cards I have made myself!

1   Which word in sentence 1 should be a plural?

Ⓐ   things

Ⓑ   likes

Ⓒ   frees

Ⓓ   times

2   In sentence 3, which word should replace *take*?

Ⓐ   took

Ⓑ   takes

Ⓒ   taken

Ⓓ   taking

3   Erin wants to add a topic sentence to the start of paragraph 2. Which of these would be the best topic sentence?

Ⓐ   I enjoy sharing my drawings with others.

Ⓑ   Drawing is an easy skill to learn.

Ⓒ   I get ideas for what to draw from many places.

Ⓓ   I once drew an elephant mother and its baby.

4   In sentence 9, which word could replace *because*?

Ⓐ   since

Ⓑ   therefore

Ⓒ   although

Ⓓ   after

5   Which of these is the best way to combine sentences 13 and 14?

Ⓐ   I don't need many supplies, it does not cost much either.

Ⓑ   I don't need many supplies, and it does not cost much either.

Ⓒ   I don't need many supplies, for it does not cost much either.

Ⓓ   I don't need many supplies, but it does not cost much either.

6   Which of these is the best way to rewrite sentence 15?

Ⓐ   I have, for my drawing supplies, a special desk in my bedroom.

Ⓑ   I have a special desk for my drawing supplies, in my bedroom.

Ⓒ   I have a special desk in my bedroom for my drawing supplies.

Ⓓ   I have in my bedroom, for my drawing supplies a special desk.

7   In sentence 21, which word should replace *which*?

    Ⓐ   her

    Ⓑ   she

    Ⓒ   who

    Ⓓ   whose

8   Which word in sentence 23 should be capitalized?

    Ⓐ   members

    Ⓑ   friday

    Ⓒ   afternoon

    Ⓓ   school

9   Which change should be made in sentence 24?

    Ⓐ   Change *there* to *their*

    Ⓑ   Change *was* to *were*

    Ⓒ   Change *who* to *which*

    Ⓓ   Change *come* to *came*

10 Which of these shows the best way to simplify sentence 27 without changing its meaning?

Ⓐ   I drew a tall giraffe with its baby giraffe.

Ⓑ   I drew a giraffe with its tall baby giraffe.

Ⓒ   I drew a giraffe, tall, with its baby giraffe.

Ⓓ   I drew a giraffe with its baby giraffe, tall.

11 Which of these shows the correct way to write sentence 28?

Ⓐ   There are some other reason' why I like drawing.

Ⓑ   There are some other reason's why I like drawing.

Ⓒ   There are some other reasons why I like drawing.

Ⓓ   There are some other reasons' why I like drawing.

12 "After all" is not the right transition phrase in sentence 32. Which phrase should replace "After all"?

Ⓐ   In my opinion

Ⓑ   In conclusion

Ⓒ   For example

Ⓓ   On the other hand

13   Which change should be made in sentence 33?

Ⓐ   Change *often* to *offen*

Ⓑ   Change *give* to *given*

Ⓒ   Change *mine* to *my*

Ⓓ   Change *too* to *two*

14   Which word should replace *bright* in sentence 34?

Ⓐ   brighten

Ⓑ   brighter

Ⓒ   brightest

Ⓓ   brightly

15   Which sentence in the last paragraph should end with a question mark?

Ⓐ   Sentence 35

Ⓑ   Sentence 37

Ⓒ   Sentence 39

Ⓓ   Sentence 40

16   In sentence 36, which word could be used in place of *calm*?

Ⓐ   excited

Ⓑ   kind

Ⓒ   relaxed

Ⓓ   thoughtful

17   In sentence 38, Erin wants to replace the words "I think" with words that show she is sure she will be drawing her whole life. Which of these shows the best words to use?

Ⓐ   If you ask me, I am certain I will be drawing my whole life!

Ⓑ   If you ask me, I believe I will be drawing my whole life!

Ⓒ   If you ask me, I truly hope I will be drawing my whole life!

Ⓓ   If you ask me, I guess I will be drawing my whole life!

18   In sentence 40, what is the correct way to spell *fammos*?

Ⓐ   famuss

Ⓑ   famous

Ⓒ   famoss

Ⓓ   famose

END OF PRACTICE SET

Passage 8

Mikhala and her friends had been practicing since the beginning of the school year for the End of the Year Talent Show. Mikhala wrote this personal narrative for the school newspaper. Read the personal narrative and look for any changes that should be made. Then answer the questions that follow.

My First Talent Show

(1) It was Friday May 5 2016. (2) That was the night of the End of the Year Talent Show. (3) My friends and I was waiting backstage. (4) I was getting more and more nervous by the minute.

(5) Then the announcer called "Rock Stars." (6) That's the name of our band. (7) We practise every Tuesday and Thursday afternoon at Tori's house. (8) My friend Margot whispered to me, "This is what we have worked so hard for. (9) Come on let's go!" (10) I smiled and nodded. (11) We very quickly ran out onto the school stage.

(12) I remember shouting into the mic. (13) "...a 1 and a 2 and 3, and hit it!" (14) Standing in the brite spotlight, I plucked the guitar strings. (15) Dad have gave me his guitar that he had when he was about my age. (16) I was so determined to do well that I could play this song with my eyes closed.

(17) To my left, I heard Toris snare drum keeping a steady beat. (18) She was dead-on. (19) And right in front, Margot sang the lyrics perfectly. (20) I was no longer nervous. (21) I felt good. (22) Just like a rock star.

(23) I looked out into the audience. (24) I could see some of my friends' faces. (25) Then I saw my dad. (26) He gave me a thumbs up. (27) Mom was smiling the wider smile I had ever seen! (28) I knew she was proud of me. (29) She was proud of all of us.

(30) When we finished our act the audience clapped. (31) "Way to go, Rock Stars!" they cheered. (32) We bowed. (33) Margot and Tori and I had done it. (34) We walked off stage.

(35) "How many more days until next year's Talent Show" Tori asked. (36) Margot and I just laughed. (37) "Let's get some ice cream," Margot suggested. (38) Sure! Tori said. (39) I quickly agreed. (40) It was certainly a night to remember!

---

(41) Note: You might wanting to perform in the Talent Show next year. (42) It's never too early to start prepairing your act. (43) Just think, you could be the next "rock stars" and have a great night!

1   Which of these shows the correct way to punctuate the date in sentence 1?

  Ⓐ   It was Friday, May 5 2016.

  Ⓑ   It was Friday May 5, 2016.

  Ⓒ   It was Friday, May 5, 2016.

  Ⓓ   It was, Friday, May 5, 2016.

2   In sentence 3, which word should replace *was*?

  Ⓐ   did

  Ⓑ   does

  Ⓒ   is

  Ⓓ   were

3   Which of these describes a change that should be made in the second paragraph to correct a spelling mistake?

  Ⓐ   Change *practise* to *practice*

  Ⓑ   Change *afternoon* to *aftenoon*

  Ⓒ   Change *whispered* to *wispered*

  Ⓓ   Change *nodded* to *noded*

4   In sentence 8, which of these shows the correct way to shorten "we have"?

Ⓐ   w've

Ⓑ   we've

Ⓒ   wev'e

Ⓓ   we'ave

5   In sentence 11, which word would best replace the phrase "very quickly ran"?

Ⓐ   followed

Ⓑ   raced

Ⓒ   shuffled

Ⓓ   wandered

6   Which change should be made in sentence 14?

Ⓐ   Change *brite* to *bright*

Ⓑ   Change *spotlight* to *spot light*

Ⓒ   Remove the comma in the sentence

Ⓓ   Replace the period with a question mark

7   In sentence 15, which words should replace "have gave me"?

Ⓐ   had give me

Ⓑ   had given me

Ⓒ   have give me

Ⓓ   have given me

8   Which change should be made in sentence 17?

Ⓐ   Change *my* to *mine*

Ⓑ   Change *heard* to *herd*

Ⓒ   Change *Toris* to *Tori's*

Ⓓ   Change *keeping* to *kept*

9   Which sentence in paragraph 4 is NOT a complete sentence?

Ⓐ   Sentence 18

Ⓑ   Sentence 20

Ⓒ   Sentence 21

Ⓓ   Sentence 22

10   Which word should replace *wider* in sentence 27?

    Ⓐ   wide

    Ⓑ   widest

    Ⓒ   widey

    Ⓓ   wideness

11   Mikhala wants to add a transition phrase to the start of sentence 29. Which of these shows the best transition phrase to use?

    Ⓐ   As a result, she was proud of all of us.

    Ⓑ   For example, she was proud of all of us.

    Ⓒ   In fact, she was proud of all of us.

    Ⓓ   All of a sudden, she was proud of all of us.

12   Which of these shows where the comma should be placed in sentence 30?

    Ⓐ   When we finished, our act the audience clapped.

    Ⓑ   When we finished our act, the audience clapped.

    Ⓒ   When we finished our act the, audience clapped.

    Ⓓ   When we finished our act the audience, clapped.

13   Sentence 35 is missing a question mark. Where should the question mark be placed in sentence 35?

    Ⓐ   "How many more days? until next year's Talent Show" Tori asked.

    Ⓑ   "How many more days until next year's Talent Show?" Tori asked.

    Ⓒ   "How many more days until next year's Talent Show"? Tori asked.

    Ⓓ   "How many more days until next year's Talent Show" Tori asked?

14   Which of these shows the correct punctuation for sentence 38?

    Ⓐ   "Sure"! Tori said.

    Ⓑ   "Sure!" Tori said.

    Ⓒ   "Sure"! Tori said."

    Ⓓ   "Sure!" Tori said."

15   As it is used in sentence 40, which word has the same meaning as *certainly*?

    Ⓐ   definitely

    Ⓑ   luckily

    Ⓒ   mostly

    Ⓓ   possibly

16   Which change should be made in sentence 41?

   Ⓐ   Change *might* to *mite*

   Ⓑ   Change *wanting* to *want*

   Ⓒ   Change *perform* to *perrform*

   Ⓓ   Change *year* to *years*

17   In sentence 42, what is the correct way to spell *prepairing*?

   Ⓐ   preparing

   Ⓑ   prepearing

   Ⓒ   preparring

   Ⓓ   prepareing

18   In sentence 43, Mikhala wants to replace "have a great night" with a more interesting phrase with about the same meaning. Which phrase would Mikhala be best to use?

   Ⓐ   have a race against time

   Ⓑ   have the time of your life

   Ⓒ   have all the time in the world

   Ⓓ   have better luck next time

END OF PRACTICE SET

Passage 9

Laura wrote this short story about a queen who liked honey. Read the short story and look for any changes that should be made. Then answer the questions that follow.

The Queen Who Loved Honey

(1) Once upon a time in a land far away, their lived a queen. (2) The queen loved to eat honey. (3) She would eat it for breckfast on her toast. (4) She would eat it at lunch on her crackers. (5) She would eat it at dinner with her yogurt. (6) Sometimes, she would just eat it plain. (7) She would unscrew the cover and just dip in her fingers.

(8) The kitchen cupboards were filled with honey jars. (9) The closets were filled with honey jars. (10) And even under her bed, there were honey jars. (11) The cook did not have to asked what the queen wanted to eat. (12) He knew the answer would every time be "honey."

(13) Well, one day the queen heard that the village amusement park was going to close. (14) She knew the park was a place that children loved to visit. (15) There were pony rides and a Ferris wheel. (16) There was a merry-go-round and a swimming pool. (17) And of course, there was cotton candy and popcorn.

(18) She wondered what the children would do without the park. (19) They would be so sad. (20) Then the queen had an idea. (21) She called for the servants to brought the horse and cart. (22) She called for the cook to collect all the honey jars. (23) There were the jars in the kitchen cupboards. (24) There were the jars in the closets. (25) There were the jars under her bed.

(26) The servants helped the cook load the jars into the cart. (27) Go and sell these at the market, the queen ordered. (28) "Then give the money to the village so the park will not close."

(29) The queen went up to her room. (30) She was happy that the children would be happy. (31) But she missed her honey. (32) Just then a yellow large bee flew into her room and it looked like it wanted to show the queen something. (33) "Okay, okay," the queen said.

(34) She ran after the bee. (35) She ran down the steps. (36) She ran out the front door. (37) She ran into the forest. (38) And there at the top of a tall tree hanged a large beehive. (39) The bee flew up and knocked its body against the hive over and over again. (40) The hive started swinging back and forth and then fell from the tree.

(41) The queen was just about to run away. (42) After all, she thought that some angry bees might come out and sting her. (43) But the bees just remarked in the hive. (44) It was like the bee was giving a gift to the queen. (45) The queen picked up the hive. (46) She walked back to her castle. (46) And then she had a snack. (47) Can you guess what she ate.

1   In sentence 1, which word should replace *their*?

Ⓐ   the

Ⓑ   they

Ⓒ   there

Ⓓ   they're

2   Which change should be made in sentence 3?

Ⓐ   Change *eat* to *eaten*

Ⓑ   Change *for* to *four*

Ⓒ   Change *breckfast* to *breakfast*

Ⓓ   Change *her* to *she*

3   Laura wants to combine sentences 8 and 9. Which of these is the best way to combine the two sentences?

Ⓐ   The kitchen cupboards and closets were filled with honey jars.

Ⓑ   The kitchen cupboards were filled with honey jars, and closets.

Ⓒ   The kitchen cupboards were filled with honey jars, closets as well.

Ⓓ   The kitchen cupboards were filled with honey jars, closets were filled with honey jars.

4   Which of these shows the correct way to rewrite sentence 11?

Ⓐ   The cook did not had to ask what the queen wanted to eat.

Ⓑ   The cook did not had to asked what the queen wanted to eat.

Ⓒ   The cook did not have to ask what the queen wanted to eat.

Ⓓ   The cook did not have to asks what the queen wanted to eat.

5   In sentence 12, which of these replaces "every time" with the best word?

Ⓐ   He knew the answer would ever be "honey."

Ⓑ   He knew the answer would always be "honey."

Ⓒ   He knew the answer would once be "honey."

Ⓓ   He knew the answer would almost be "honey."

6   Sentence 14 can express the same meaning, but be written in a simpler way. Which of these shows the best way to rewrite sentence 14 without changing its meaning?

Ⓐ   She loved to visit the park with her children.

Ⓑ   She knew that children loved to visit the park.

Ⓒ   The park was loved to visit by children.

Ⓓ   Of all the places children went, the park was loved, she knew.

7   Which of these shows the best way to combine sentences 15 and 16?

Ⓐ   There were pony rides, a Ferris wheel, a merry-go-round, and a swimming pool.

Ⓑ   There were pony rides and a Ferris wheel, and a merry-go-round and a swimming pool.

Ⓒ   There were pony rides, Ferris wheel, merry-go-round, swimming pool.

Ⓓ   There were pony rides, and a Ferris wheel, and a merry-go-round, and a swimming pool.

8   In sentence 21, which word should replace *brought*?

Ⓐ   bring

Ⓑ   brings

Ⓒ   bought

Ⓓ   bringing

9   Which of these shows the correct way to use quotation marks in sentence 27?

Ⓐ   "Go and sell these" at the market, the queen ordered.

Ⓑ   "Go and sell these at the market," the queen ordered.

Ⓒ   "Go and sell these at the market," the queen ordered."

Ⓓ   "Go and sell these at the market, the queen ordered."

10   Which word could be added to the end of sentence 31 to show how much the queen missed the honey?

Ⓐ   bad

Ⓑ   badly

Ⓒ   baddest

Ⓓ   badness

11   In sentence 32, what is the more common order for the words "yellow large bee"?

Ⓐ   large yellow bee

Ⓑ   bee yellow large

Ⓒ   large bee yellow

Ⓓ   bee large yellow

12   Which of these shows the best way to combine sentences 35, 36, and 37?

Ⓐ   She ran down the steps, front door, and forest.

Ⓑ   She ran down the steps, out the front door, into the forest.

Ⓒ   She ran down the steps, out the front door, and into the forest.

Ⓓ   She ran down the steps, she ran out the front door, she ran into the forest.

13   Which word should replace *hanged* in sentence 38?

 Ⓐ hang

 Ⓑ hung

 Ⓒ hangs

 Ⓓ hanging

14   In sentence 39, which word could replace "over and over again"?

 Ⓐ reportedly

 Ⓑ repeatedly

 Ⓒ respectfully

 Ⓓ responsibly

15   Laura wants to improve sentence 40 by adding a detail at the end that helps the reader imagine the hive landing on the ground with a heavy dull sound. Which of these shows the best way to end the sentence to achieve this?

 Ⓐ The hive started swinging back and forth and then fell from the tree with a ping.

 Ⓑ The hive started swinging back and forth and then fell from the tree with a buzz.

 Ⓒ The hive started swinging back and forth and then fell from the tree with a clang.

 Ⓓ The hive started swinging back and forth and then fell from the tree with a thud.

16   In sentence 41, which word could replace *run* to show that the queen wanted to run away fast?

    Ⓐ   bolt

    Ⓑ   sneak

    Ⓒ   stroll

    Ⓓ   wander

17   In sentence 43, *remarked* is not the right word. Which word should be used to show that the bees stayed in the hive?

    Ⓐ   reminded

    Ⓑ   removed

    Ⓒ   remained

    Ⓓ   rematched

18   Which sentence in the last paragraph should end with a question mark?

    Ⓐ   Sentence 41

    Ⓑ   Sentence 42

    Ⓒ   Sentence 46

    Ⓓ   Sentence 47

END OF PRACTICE SET

Passage 10

The students in Jason's class were asked to write an opinion article about how to improve transportation methods for their city. Jason wrote this article about a bike-sharing program. Read the article and look for any changes that should be made. Then answer the questions that follow.

Why We Should Have a Bike-Sharing Program

(1) We can improve transportation in our comunity with a bike-sharing program. (2) Many of my friends and family members needs another way to get to work and school. (3) Although our city offers buses, the buses only help a little. (4) I think the best way to help our city is to create a bike-sharing program.

(5) A bike-sharing program would help the people access the buses too. (6) We could travel to the city center without problems if we had bikes. (7) I think a bike-sharing system is better then adding more bus routes. (8) It will also cost the city less money. (9) A bike-sharing program can cost less money to begin than making more train tracks. (10) Starting a bike-sharing program will help everyone get to work and school. (11) It can cost the citizens less money than taking the bus.

(12) Many of the people in our neighborhood need public transportation. (13) Their neighborhoods are not all contacted to the bus routes. (14) Sometimes we need to go from one neighborhood to another, and there is no bus that is close. (15) Having many bikes available through a bike-sharing program will make it more easy for everyone to get where they want to go.

(16) If we had a bike-sharing program in our city we also don't have to wait for the bus. (17) Sometimes the bus is late and it makes me late to school. (18) When the bus is late it makes my mother late to work too. (19) In bad weather, most people cannot use bicycles, but our city has short winters. (20) I think a bike-sharing program can help everyone during the year. (21) If we had a bike-sharing program, my mother could meet me at school on a bicycle. (22) Then we could ride the bikes home together.

(23) Our city has a lot of traffic, and it is difficult to get to school during the week. (24) In fact, it is often hard to travel anywhere in the city. (25) Traffic is causing a lots of problems. (26) There are lots of car accidents, I am always hearing about them on the news. (27) Using a bike-sharing program can help us reduce traffic. (28) Maybe it can reduce the how many accidents there are.

(29) I think that a bike-sharing program is the best option for our city for everyone. (30) A bike-sharing program can save everyone time and money.

If more people traveled by bike, there would be fewer cars on the road and less traffic.

1   In sentence 1, what is the correct way to spell *comunity*?

   Ⓐ   community

   Ⓑ   comunnity

   Ⓒ   communitty

   Ⓓ   comunitie

2   In sentence 2, which of these should replace *needs*?

   Ⓐ   need

   Ⓑ   needing

   Ⓒ   has needed

   Ⓓ   is needing

3   Jason wants to revise sentence 3 so that it doesn't use the phrase "the buses" twice. Which of these shows the word that should replace the second use of "the buses"?

   Ⓐ   Although our city offers buses, she only help a little.

   Ⓑ   Although our city offers buses, them only help a little.

   Ⓒ   Although our city offers buses, they only help a little.

   Ⓓ   Although our city offers buses, we only help a little.

4   Which change should be made in sentence 7?

ⓐ   Change *better* to *best*

ⓑ   Change *then* to *than*

ⓒ   Change *adding* to *ading*

ⓓ   Change *more* to *most*

5   Jason wants to replace the word *can* in sentence 9 to make the savings described seem more certain. Which word would Jason be best to use to create a sense of certainty?

ⓐ   could

ⓑ   may

ⓒ   should

ⓓ   will

6   Which word can be removed from sentence 11 without changing its meaning?

ⓐ   can

ⓑ   less

ⓒ   money

ⓓ   bus

7   In sentence 13, *contacted* is not the right word. Which word meaning "joined or linked together" should be used in place of *contacted*?

Ⓐ   concluded

Ⓑ   controlled

Ⓒ   connected

Ⓓ   continued

8   In sentence 14, which word should replace *and*?

Ⓐ   but

Ⓑ   for

Ⓒ   or

Ⓓ   so

9   In sentence 15, which word should replace "more easy"?

Ⓐ   easier

Ⓑ   easily

Ⓒ   easiest

Ⓓ   easiness

10   In sentence 16, which word would be the best replacement for *don't*?

Ⓐ   didn't

Ⓑ   wouldn't

Ⓒ   aren't

Ⓓ   doesn't

11   Which of these shows where the comma should be placed in sentence 18?

Ⓐ   When the bus, is late it makes my mother late to work too.

Ⓑ   When the bus is late, it makes my mother late to work too.

Ⓒ   When the bus is late it makes my mother, late to work too.

Ⓓ   When the bus is late it makes my mother late, to work too.

12   Jason wants to add a sentence before sentence 23 to introduce the ideas in the paragraph. Which sentence would Jason be best to add?

Ⓐ   A bike-sharing program could even help solve traffic problems.

Ⓑ   Heavy traffic often makes people very upset.

Ⓒ   If you plan when you travel, you can avoid traffic problems.

Ⓓ   People could have accidents while riding.

13   Which of these shows how sentence 23 could be rewritten to better show the relationship between the ideas?

Ⓐ   It is difficult to get to school during the week because our city has a lot of traffic.

Ⓑ   It is difficult to get to school during the week until our city has a lot of traffic.

Ⓒ   It is difficult to get to school during the week after our city has a lot of traffic.

Ⓓ   It is difficult to get to school during the week always our city has a lot of traffic.

14   Which of these shows the correct way to write sentence 25?

Ⓐ   Traffic is causing a lot of problem.

Ⓑ   Traffic is causing a lot's of problem.

Ⓒ   Traffic is causing a lot of problems.

Ⓓ   Traffic is causing a lot of problem's.

15   Jason wants to add a supporting detail after sentence 25 to support the idea that traffic is causing lots of problems. Which sentence would Jason be best to use?

Ⓐ   Traffic occurs when there are too many cars in one place.

Ⓑ   I avoid traffic problems by riding my bike.

Ⓒ   Traffic annoys people and causes a lot of stress.

Ⓓ   One way to avoid traffic is simply to stay home.

16   Sentence 26 is not written correctly. Which of these shows the best way to rewrite the sentence in a simpler way?

Ⓐ   There are lots of car accidents I am hearing about on the news.

Ⓑ   The news I am always hearing about is lots of car accidents.

Ⓒ   The car accidents on the news, lots of them I am hearing about.

Ⓓ   I am always hearing about lots of car accidents on the news.

17   Which word should be removed from sentence 28?

Ⓐ   it

Ⓑ   can

Ⓒ   the

Ⓓ   there

18   In sentence 29, Jason wants to replace *think* with a stronger word. Which word would best show that Jason strongly believes that the bike-sharing program is a good option?

Ⓐ   hope

Ⓑ   know

Ⓒ   imagine

Ⓓ   wonder

END OF PRACTICE SET

Passage 11

Mary's class was asked to choose any of the Seven Wonders of the World and write about it. Mary chose to write a report about the Hanging Gardens of Babylon. Read the report and look for any changes that should be made. Then answer the questions that follow.

The Hanging Gardens of Babylon

(1) The Hanging Gardens of Babylon is the only one that may not have actually existed in the Seven Wonders of the World. (2) It is still part of the Seven Wonders because it was believed that the gardens were destroyed. (3) It is known as the Hanging Gardens because the gardens were built high on different levels of stone terraces. (4) It was described as the most beautyful man-made gardens. (5) The gardens also had flowers fruits waterfalls and exotic creatures. (6) There may even have been big vaults and arches inside it.

(7) Roman and greek writers have written about the gardens in many classic works. (8) They described how and why it was created and how large the gardens were. (9) Not any the writers agreed on why they were built and who they were built for. (10) A populer idea is that the gardens were made by King Nebuchadnezzar II because it was built near a royal palace. (11) He made the Hanging Gardens to make his sick wife happyer.

(12) Another idea was that the Queen Sammu-ramat built the gardens with she husband, Nimrod. (13) She was knowed as the mother of the Assyrian king, Adad-Nirari III. (14) The Assyrian king ruled from 810 BC to 783 BC. (15) They believed that Sammu-ramat and Nimrod built the gardens because they founded Babylon. (16) It was also believed that they made them because they looked after other buildings created in Babylon.

(17) The gardens is said to be 400 feet by 400 feet long. (18) Watering the plants would take over 8,000 gallons of water every single day. (19) They were raised 75 feet high. (20) Because the gardens were so high the water would need to be carried up before you can water them. (21) It is said that three strange holes in the bottom of the gardens made watering the plants easier. (22) The water for the gardens was supposed to come from the euphrates river.

(23) Even though they are called The Hanging Gardens of Babylon, it is believed that they would actually have been in Iraq. (24) Nineveh is the closest to Babylon that could have made such a garden. (25) Nineveh is an ancient city located in modern-day Iraq.

(26) The Hanging Gardens of Babylon are still being argued about. (27) There is not enough proof that they really existed. (28) They may have actually come from the imaginations of writers and poets. (29) It may never be known weather it was ever real, or is purely a wonderful work of fiction.

This picture shows an artwork created in the 1800s. It shows what the Hanging Gardens of Babylon are thought to have looked like.

1   Sentence 1 can be reorganized to make the meaning clearer. Which of these shows the best way to rewrite sentence 1?

Ⓐ   The only one that may not have actually existed in the Seven Wonders of the World is the Hanging Gardens of Babylon.

Ⓑ   In the Seven Wonders of the World is the only one that may not have actually existed, the Hanging Gardens of Babylon.

Ⓒ   The Hanging Gardens of Babylon is the only one of the Seven Wonders of the World that may not have actually existed.

Ⓓ   It may not have actually existed in the Seven Wonders of the World, the Hanging Gardens of Babylon.

2   In sentence 4, what is the correct way to write *beautyful*?

Ⓐ   beautiful

Ⓑ   beauttiful

Ⓒ   beautyfull

Ⓓ   beautifull

3   Which of these shows the correct use of commas in sentence 5?

Ⓐ   The gardens also had flowers fruits waterfalls, and exotic creatures.

Ⓑ   The gardens also had flowers, fruits, waterfalls, and exotic creatures.

Ⓒ   The gardens also had flowers, fruits, waterfalls, and exotic, creatures.

Ⓓ   The gardens also had, flowers, fruits, waterfalls, and exotic creatures.

4   In sentence 6, which word could replace *big* to emphasize the large size of the vaults?

Ⓐ   slender

Ⓑ   massive

Ⓒ   narrow

Ⓓ   sturdy

5   Which word in sentence 7 should be capitalized?

Ⓐ   greek

Ⓑ   writers

Ⓒ   classic

Ⓓ   works

6   In sentence 9, which word should replace *any*?

Ⓐ   all

Ⓑ   every

Ⓒ   many

Ⓓ   most

7 Which change should be made in sentence 10?

Ⓐ Change *populer* to *popular*

Ⓑ Change *gardens* to *garden's*

Ⓒ Change *near* to *nearby*

Ⓓ Change *palace* to *palase*

8 In sentence 11, which of these should replace *happyer*?

Ⓐ hapyer

Ⓑ hapier

Ⓒ happier

Ⓓ happyier

9 In sentence 12, which word should replace *she*?

Ⓐ her

Ⓑ him

Ⓒ its

Ⓓ their

10   In sentence 13, which word should replace *knowed*?

   Ⓐ   know

   Ⓑ   knows

   Ⓒ   known

   Ⓓ   knowing

11   In sentence 14, which meaning of the word *ruled* is used?

   Ⓐ   Was in charge of

   Ⓑ   Marked with lines

   Ⓒ   Made a decision

   Ⓓ   Better than others

12   In sentence 17, the word *is* should not be used. Which of these shows the correct word to replace *is* with?

   Ⓐ   The gardens am said to be 400 feet by 400 feet long.

   Ⓑ   The gardens was said to be 400 feet by 400 feet long.

   Ⓒ   The gardens did said to be 400 feet by 400 feet long.

   Ⓓ   The gardens were said to be 400 feet by 400 feet long.

13   Which sentence in paragraph 4 would best be changed to end with an exclamation mark?

Ⓐ   Sentence 18

Ⓑ   Sentence 20

Ⓒ   Sentence 21

Ⓓ   Sentence 22

14   Which of these shows the correct placement of a comma in sentence 20?

Ⓐ   Because, the gardens were so high the water would need to be carried up before you can water them.

Ⓑ   Because the gardens, were so high the water would need to be carried up before you can water them.

Ⓒ   Because the gardens were so high, the water would need to be carried up before you can water them.

Ⓓ   Because the gardens were so high the water, would need to be carried up before you can water them.

15   Which of these shows the correct use of capitals in sentence 22?

Ⓐ   The water for the gardens was supposed to come from the Euphrates river.

Ⓑ   The Water for the gardens was supposed to come from the Euphrates river.

Ⓒ   The water for the gardens was supposed to come from the Euphrates River.

Ⓓ   The Water for the gardens was supposed to come from the Euphrates River.

16   Which of these shows the correct way to combine the ideas in sentences 24 and 25?

    Ⓐ   Nineveh, is an ancient city located in modern-day Iraq, is the closest to Babylon that could have made such a garden.

    Ⓑ   Nineveh, which is an ancient city located in modern-day Iraq, is the closest to Babylon that could have made such a garden.

    Ⓒ   Nineveh is the closest to Babylon that could have made such a garden, is an ancient city located in modern-day Iraq.

    Ⓓ   Nineveh is the closest to Babylon that could have made such a garden, which is an ancient city located in modern-day Iraq.

17   In sentence 26, which word would best replace "argued about"?

    Ⓐ   chatted

    Ⓑ   created

    Ⓒ   debated

    Ⓓ   wondered

18   Which change should be made in sentence 29?

    Ⓐ   Replace *weather* with *whether*

    Ⓑ   Replace *purely* with *pure*

    Ⓒ   Replace *wonderful* with *wonderfull*

    Ⓓ   Replace *fiction* with *fictional*

END OF PRACTICE SET

Passage 12

Nikki's teacher asked her to write an opinion piece about something she is passionate about. Nikki decided to write an essay arguing that dance should be considered a sport. Read the opinion piece and look for any changes that should be made. Then answer the questions that follow.

Dance as a Sport

(1) Many people argue over either or not dance should be considered a sport. (2) Despite the debate, dance should certainly be considered a sport. (3) Dance requires training, strength and stamina, and can include competition. (4) As a whole, dance should always be seen and treated as a sport.

(5) Training is one of the most important parts of dance. (6) Dancers spend countless hours in the studio practiceing. (7) Dance teachers are a lot like coaches in a sport. (8) Teachers train dancers to improve and create routines for it to perform. (9) These routines can be compared to plays in a football game. (10) Both football players and dancers are given a plan to carry out in order to succeed in they're sport. (11) Training is also a lot like practices. (12) Dancers practice by working on technique just like any other organized sport. (13) Overall, training and practices in dance are the same as other hobbies that are considered sports.

(14) Another reason dance should be defined as a sport is the strength and stamina that is required of the dancers. (15) Dancers must be in good physical shape to perform and are constant working towards strongest muscles. (16) A dance routine can last anywhere from a few seconds – several minutes. (17) This demands extra stamina of the dancers. (18) Basketball players for instance are always trying to increase their stamina. (19) The basketball games require players to run back and forth across the court almost constantly. (20) Both dancers and basketball players must build strength and stamina to play good in their sports.

Ballet dancers require great strength, and also need to be fit enough to keep dancing.

(21) Additionally, dance often includes competition. (22) Some people say that dance is not a sport because there are no games. (23) In reality, there are loads of dancers who compete. (24) The award winning dance show *Dancing with the Stars* is just one example of these competitions. (25) There are many more competitions for dancers of all styles. (26) These range from small local contests to major national and international competitions.

(27) Just as a soccer championship involves multiple games, dance competitions can involve multiple performances. (28) Dancers may perform as a group, as well. (29) This group of dancers resembles the average soccer team with different athletes filling different roles. (30) Competitive dancers are definitely athletes. (31) Dance should be considered a sport.

(32) In conclusion, dance has many aspects that are similer to typical sports. (33) Dancers are always practicing, gaining strength and stamina, and most compete regular. (34) In the debate of whether dance is a sport, the answer seems pretty clear. (35) Dance is undoubtedly a sport.

1   In sentence 1, which word should replace *either*?

Ⓐ   always

Ⓑ   ever

Ⓒ   neither

Ⓓ   whether

2   In sentence 4, Nikki wants to replace "As a whole" with a single transition word that has the same meaning. Which transition word would Nikki be best to use?

Ⓐ   However

Ⓑ   Overall

Ⓒ   Otherwise

Ⓓ   Still

3   Which change should be made in sentence 6?

Ⓐ   Change *spend* to *spending*

Ⓑ   Change *countless* to *count less*

Ⓒ   Change *hours* to *hour's*

Ⓓ   Change *practiceing* to *practicing*

4   In sentence 8, which word should replace *it*?

Ⓐ   them

Ⓑ   they

Ⓒ   these

Ⓓ   those

5   Which change should be made in sentence 10?

Ⓐ   Replace *given* with *gave*

Ⓑ   Replace *to* with *too*

Ⓒ   Replace *succeed* with *succede*

Ⓓ   Replace *they're* with *their*

6   Which of these shows the correct way to write sentence 15?

Ⓐ   Dancers must be in good physical shape to perform and are constant working towards stronger muscles.

Ⓑ   Dancers must be in good physical shape to perform and are constant working towards strongly muscles.

Ⓒ   Dancers must be in good physical shape to perform and are constantly working towards stronger muscles.

Ⓓ   Dancers must be in good physical shape to perform and are constantly working towards strongly muscles.

7   Which of these shows the correct word to replace the dash in sentence 16?

Ⓐ   A dance routine can last anywhere from a few seconds and several minutes.

Ⓑ   A dance routine can last anywhere from a few seconds or several minutes.

Ⓒ   A dance routine can last anywhere from a few seconds to several minutes.

Ⓓ   A dance routine can last anywhere from a few seconds with several minutes.

8   Which of these shows the correct placement of commas in sentence 18?

Ⓐ   Basketball players, for instance, are always trying to increase their stamina.

Ⓑ   Basketball players, for instance are always, trying to increase their stamina.

Ⓒ   Basketball players for instance are, always trying, to increase their stamina.

Ⓓ   Basketball players for instance are, always trying to increase, their stamina.

9   In sentence 20, which word should replace *good*?

Ⓐ   best

Ⓑ   nice

Ⓒ   more

Ⓓ   well

10   Nikki wants to add a sentence to the end of paragraph 3 to bring it to a better close. Which sentence would Nikki be best to add?

Ⓐ   As you can see, dancers need strength and stamina just like other sportspeople.

Ⓑ   Ballet dancers may look lean, but they actually need to be very strong as well.

Ⓒ   Champion basketball players never seem to get tired because they have worked hard on their stamina.

Ⓓ   Strength refers to how strong someone is, while stamina refers to how long someone can keep going.

11   In sentence 23, Nikki wants to replace "loads of" with a word that sounds more formal. Which word should Nikki use that means about the same as "loads of"?

Ⓐ   any

Ⓑ   few

Ⓒ   many

Ⓓ   some

12   Which two words in sentence 24 should be joined with a hyphen?

Ⓐ   award-winning

Ⓑ   dance-show

Ⓒ   one-example

Ⓓ   these-competitions

13 Nikki wants to add a sentence after sentence 26 to give an example that supports the ideas in sentence 26. Which sentence would Nikki be best to add?

Ⓐ For example, you have to train hard to win contests.

Ⓑ For example, the National Ballroom Championships are held every year.

Ⓒ For example, it can also be fun just to dance because you enjoy it.

Ⓓ For example, dancers competing on television can become famous.

14 In sentence 27, the word *multiple* is used twice. Which word could replace the second use of *multiple* without changing the meaning of the sentence?

Ⓐ difficult

Ⓑ long

Ⓒ many

Ⓓ more

15 Nikki wants to add a transition word to the start of sentence 31 to better connect sentences 30 and 31. Which of these shows the transition word that Nikki would be best to use?

Ⓐ However, dance should be considered a sport.

Ⓑ Usually, dance should be considered a sport.

Ⓒ Meanwhile, dance should be considered a sport.

Ⓓ Therefore, dance should be considered a sport.

16   Which change should be made in sentence 32?

ⓐ   Change *has* to *have*

ⓑ   Change *aspects* to *aspect*

ⓒ   Change *similer* to *similar*

ⓓ   Change *typical* to *typicel*

17   Which change should be made in sentence 33?

ⓐ   Change *practicing* to *practice*

ⓑ   Change *gaining* to *gained*

ⓒ   Change *compete* to *competes*

ⓓ   Change *regular* to *regularly*

18   In sentence 34, which word would be the best replacement for "pretty clear"?

ⓐ   bright

ⓑ   obvious

ⓒ   perfect

ⓓ   strong

END OF PRACTICE SET

Passage 13

Alice and her classmates were asked to write about a time when they argued with someone and what happened after. Alice wrote about the time she argued with her best friend Lily. Read the personal narrative and look for any changes that should be made. Then answer the questions that follow.

A Fight with my Best Friend

(1) When I was 7 years old, I was best friends with girl named Lily. (2) She did not go to my school, she used to live next door. (3) She have moved away now. (4) We used to play toggether every day after school. (5) Her mom used to work late, so Lily always stays at my house until her mom came home. (6) In many ways, it felt like we was sisters.

(7) I remember that mine mom bought me a lovely set of new hair clips. (8) She gave them to me when I got home from school and told me to take care of them. (9) She then saided she would be busy working and went into her office.

(10) When Lily arrived, I was excited to show her my new hair clips. (11) That was when Lily decidded to play hairdressers. (12) She told me that I would be the hairdresser, she customer. (13) I had so much fun combing her hair and placing the new hair clips in. (14) I asked Lily if she liked her hairstyle and she said she loved it very much. (15) She then suggested to play another game and we continued having fun.

(16) After a while Lily's mom knocked on our door to fetch her. (17) Lily ran to her mom and said goodbye to me. (18) I asked her to return the hair clips and she told me she wouldnt. (19) She explained that I had given them to her as a gift. (20) I cried and asked and asked my mom to get them back for me. (21) Lily had already told her mom that I gave her my hair clips and that she really wanted them. (22) She started crying then, too. (23) In the end, my mom let her keep the hair clips and then scolded me afterwards for giving away things that have been given to me.

(24) Lily still came to my house every day but she didn't wear the hair clips then. (25) One day, she gave them back to me when they was all worn out. (26) She told me she didn't want them anymore and that I could have them back. (27) Lily was a bit selfish, and I'm still glad I didn't let hair clips ruin our friendship.

1   In sentence 1, a word needs to be added before *girl*. Which of these shows the correct word to add?

    Ⓐ   When I was 7 years old, I was best friends with my girl named Lily.

    Ⓑ   When I was 7 years old, I was best friends with an girl named Lily.

    Ⓒ   When I was 7 years old, I was best friends with the girl named Lily.

    Ⓓ   When I was 7 years old, I was best friends with a girl named Lily.

2   In sentence 2, which of these shows the best word to add after the comma?

    Ⓐ   She did not go to my school, so she used to live next door.

    Ⓑ   She did not go to my school, for she used to live next door.

    Ⓒ   She did not go to my school, but she used to live next door.

    Ⓓ   She did not go to my school, or she used to live next door.

3   Which of these shows the correct way to write sentence 3?

    Ⓐ   She has moved away now.

    Ⓑ   She having moved away now.

    Ⓒ   She will have moved away now.

    Ⓓ   She have move away now.

4   In sentence 4, what is the correct way to spell *toggether*?

    Ⓐ   together

    Ⓑ   togethor

    Ⓒ   toogether

    Ⓓ   toogethor

5   In sentence 5, which word should replace *stays*?

    Ⓐ   stay

    Ⓑ   stayed

    Ⓒ   stayer

    Ⓓ   staying

6   Which change should be made in sentence 6?

    Ⓐ   Replace *ways* with *way*

    Ⓑ   Replace *felt* with *feeled*

    Ⓒ   Replace *was* with *were*

    Ⓓ   Replace *sisters* with *sister's*

7   Which change should be made in sentence 7?

    Ⓐ   Change *mine* to *my*

    Ⓑ   Change *bought* to *buy*

    Ⓒ   Change *lovely* to *lovelly*

    Ⓓ   Change *new* to *knew*

8   In sentence 9, *saided* is not a real word. Which word should be used in place of *saided*?

    Ⓐ   say

    Ⓑ   says

    Ⓒ   saying

    Ⓓ   said

9   In sentence 11, what is the correct way to spell *decidded*?

    Ⓐ   decided

    Ⓑ   desidded

    Ⓒ   desided

    Ⓓ   decidered

10   The end of sentence 12 is not written correctly. Which of these shows how to write the sentence correctly?

Ⓐ   She told me that I would be the hairdresser, and she customer.

Ⓑ   She told me that I would be the hairdresser, and she be customer.

Ⓒ   She told me that I would be the hairdresser, and she be the customer.

Ⓓ   She told me that I would be the hairdresser, and she would be the customer.

11   Alice wants to change the end of sentence 14 to describe how much Lily liked the hairstyle in a simpler way. Which of these shows the best way to end the sentence without changing its meaning?

Ⓐ   I asked Lily if she liked her hairstyle and she said she accepted it.

Ⓑ   I asked Lily if she liked her hairstyle and she said she adored it.

Ⓒ   I asked Lily if she liked her hairstyle and she said she disliked it.

Ⓓ   I asked Lily if she liked her hairstyle and she said she wanted it.

12   In sentence 15, which word should replace "to play"?

Ⓐ   play

Ⓑ   plays

Ⓒ   played

Ⓓ   playing

13   Which of these shows where a comma should be placed in sentence 16?

  Ⓐ   After, a while Lily's mom knocked on our door to fetch her.

  Ⓑ   After a while, Lily's mom knocked on our door to fetch her.

  Ⓒ   After a while Lily's mom, knocked on our door to fetch her.

  Ⓓ   After a while Lily's mom knocked on our door, to fetch her.

14   In sentence 18, which of these shows where the apostrophe should be placed in *wouldnt*?

  Ⓐ   woul'dnt

  Ⓑ   would'nt

  Ⓒ   wouldn't

  Ⓓ   wouldnt'

15   In sentence 20, Alice uses the words "asked and asked" to show how strongly she asked her mother to help her. Which of these would be a better word to use in place of "asked and asked"?

  Ⓐ   begged

  Ⓑ   hoped

  Ⓒ   talked

  Ⓓ   yelled

16   In sentence 23, which transition word could be used in place of "In the end"?

    Ⓐ   Finally

    Ⓑ   However

    Ⓒ   Overall

    Ⓓ   Therefore

17   In sentence 25, which word should replace *was*?

    Ⓐ   are

    Ⓑ   be

    Ⓒ   is

    Ⓓ   were

18   In sentence 27, *and* is not the best word to use after the comma. Which word would be best to use in place of *and*?

    Ⓐ   but

    Ⓑ   for

    Ⓒ   or

    Ⓓ   so

END OF PRACTICE SET

Passage 14

In science class, Grace had been learning about rocks. Her science teacher asked her to write a fictional piece about a rock's journey down a river during a flood. She wrote the following story. Read the story and look for any changes that should be made. Then answer the questions that follow.

A Little Rock's Journey

(1) I started my life as part of a really big rock. (2) I lived next to a long and winding peacefull river. (3) After some time, I fell from mother rock and landed safely on the sand below. (4) I sat quietly on this bit of sand for a long time.

(5) It was truly a wonderful spot. (6) In the day, I was shaded by a huge tree. (7) At night, I could here the water of the river moving past the shore.

(8) Then one day, it started to rain. (9) It just kept on raining and raining. (10) The river level rose higher and higher. (11) Eventually I was picked up in the flood waters and carried away.

(12) On my journey down the river, I saw many things that were amazing. (13) As I rolled over and over on the river bed, I saw many interesting animals. (14) I saw many fish crayfish and turtles.

(15) One time, a large fish was feeding on the little creatures on the river bed. (16) Every time the fish picked up some food it would pick up some sand and pebbles too. (17) It would spit out anything it didn't want to eaten back into the water.

(18) The fish dived down in my direction and took a big gulp. (19) Suddenly, I was in the mouth of the fish. (20) Thankfully, it spat me out into the water. (21) I drifted gentle to the bottom again.

(22) The currents continued to carry me downstream. (23) I bumped into many rocks and sticks along the way.

(24) One day I went through some rapids. (25) The rapids was very strong and threw me around in the water. (26) Being tossed about like that was actually quite fun.

(27) After three day of traveling down the river, I came to rest next to a big sturdy log. (28) The rain stopped and the flood waters slowly went down. (29) I now had a new home. (30) It was a beautiful spot. (31) It was next to some nice big rocks and colorful trees. (32) Sometimes a nice breeze would sweep over me during the day.

(33) After a long journey down the river, my outside surface was nice and smooth. (34) I looked like all the river pebbles around me and felt quite at home. (35) It was great to make some new friends and see lots of new animals. (36) I look forward to my next journey downstream.

1   Grace wants to replace the words "really big" in sentence 1 with a single word
         that has the same meaning. Which word should Grace use?

         Ⓐ   central

         Ⓑ   massive

         Ⓒ   minute

         Ⓓ   wonderful

2   Which of these describes a spelling error that needs to be corrected in
         paragraph 1?

         Ⓐ   Change *winding* to *windeing*

         Ⓑ   Change *peacefull* to *peaceful*

         Ⓒ   Change *safely* to *safelly*

         Ⓓ   Change *quietly* to *quiettly*

3   In sentence 7, Grace has made an error and used the wrong homophone for one
         of the words. Which change should be made to correct the error?

         Ⓐ   Change *night* to *knight*

         Ⓑ   Change *here* to *hear*

         Ⓒ   Change *past* to *passed*

         Ⓓ   Change *shore* to *sure*

4   In sentence 8, which word could replace *started*?

 Ⓐ began

 Ⓑ begun

 Ⓒ begins

 Ⓓ beginning

5   Which of these shows where the comma should be placed in sentence 11?

 Ⓐ Eventually, I was picked up in the flood waters and carried away.

 Ⓑ Eventually I was picked, up in the flood waters and carried away.

 Ⓒ Eventually I was picked up, in the flood waters and carried away.

 Ⓓ Eventually I was picked up in the flood waters, and carried away.

6   Sentence 12 can be rewritten in a simpler way. Which of these shows the best way to rewrite sentence 12?

 Ⓐ On my journey down the river, amazing I saw many things.

 Ⓑ On my journey down the river, I saw amazing many things.

 Ⓒ On my journey down the river, I saw many amazing things.

 Ⓓ On my journey down the river, I saw many things amazing.

7   Which of these shows how commas should be placed in sentence 14?

Ⓐ   I saw many fish crayfish, and turtles.

Ⓑ   I saw many, fish crayfish, and turtles.

Ⓒ   I saw many fish, crayfish, and turtles.

Ⓓ   I saw many fish, crayfish, and, turtles.

8   In sentence 15, which word could be used to start the sentence in place of "One time"?

Ⓐ   Once

Ⓑ   Finally

Ⓒ   Suddenly

Ⓓ   Then

9   In sentence 17, which word should replace *eaten*?

Ⓐ   ate

Ⓑ   eat

Ⓒ   eats

Ⓓ   eating

10   Which sentence in paragraph 6 would be best to end with an exclamation mark?

   Ⓐ   Sentence 18

   Ⓑ   Sentence 19

   Ⓒ   Sentence 20

   Ⓓ   Sentence 21

11   In sentence 21, which word should replace *gentle*?

   Ⓐ   gently

   Ⓑ   gentler

   Ⓒ   gentled

   Ⓓ   gentlest

12   In Sentence 25, which word should replace *was*?

   Ⓐ   are

   Ⓑ   be

   Ⓒ   is

   Ⓓ   were

13   Grace wants to add a transition word to the start of sentence 26. Which of these shows the best transition word to use?

Ⓐ   Shockingly, being tossed about like that was actually quite fun.

Ⓑ   Sadly, being tossed about like that was actually quite fun.

Ⓒ   Surprisingly, being tossed about like that was actually quite fun.

Ⓓ   Suddenly, being tossed about like that was actually quite fun.

14   Which word in sentence 27 should be a plural?

Ⓐ   day

Ⓑ   river

Ⓒ   rest

Ⓓ   log

15   A dictionary entry for the word *spot* is shown below.

> **spot** *noun* 1. a small round mark 2. a certain place or point
> 3. a small amount of something 4. a pimple

Which meaning of the word *spot* is used in sentence 30?

Ⓐ   Meaning 1

Ⓑ   Meaning 2

Ⓒ   Meaning 3

Ⓓ   Meaning 4

16   In sentence 34, *feeled* is not a real word. Which word should be used in place of *feeled*?

    Ⓐ   feel

    Ⓑ   felt

    Ⓒ   felted

    Ⓓ   feeling

17   Grace wants to add the following sentence to the last paragraph.

    The moving water had worn away all my rough edges.

Which of these is the best place to add the sentence?

    Ⓐ   After sentence 33

    Ⓑ   After sentence 34

    Ⓒ   After sentence 35

    Ⓓ   After sentence 36

18   Grace wants to add the word *truly* to sentence 36 to emphasize the pebble's strong feelings. Which of these shows the best way to add the word?

    Ⓐ   I truly look forward to my next journey downstream.

    Ⓑ   I look forward truly to my next journey downstream.

    Ⓒ   I look forward to truly my next journey downstream.

    Ⓓ   I look forward to my next journey downstream truly.

END OF PRACTICE SET

Passage 15

Deena was asked to write about a personal experience for her English class. She wrote the following personal narrative about her first day at a new school. Read the personal narrative and look for any changes that should be made. Then answer the questions that follow.

My First Day at Mayfield Primary School

(1) Some time ago, my family moved into a new house. (2) Because we moved I had to change schools. (3) When my mom told me I was going to a new school, I was very afraid. (4) I had good friends at my old school. (5) I would now have to make new ones.

(6) My first day of school was a bit scarey. (7) I didn't know anybody – not even the teachers. (8) When I got showed around the school I tried to remember where everything was. (9) But later I forgot. (10) It was difficult for me to ask for directions.

(11) I had to get used to my new class and classmates. (12) My new class looked very different. (13) I also have to start learning new things and catching up on some work that I missed. (14) I put up my hand when I was unsure about something and the teacher helped me a lot. (15) She was very kind and gave me lot of help.

(16) At lunchtime, I wasn't sure wear to sit. (17) At first, I sat on my own, so then Brianna came and asked me to sit with her friends. (18) They were an awesome group of people and they made me feel welcome. (19) Brianna answered any questions I had and tell me about all the fun things that happen at the school. (20) I really appreciated her help. (21) We also played some games that were fun at lunch.

(22) After school, Dad left work early and came to pick me up. (23) He asked me how my day is. (24) I told he that my first day at school was a bit frightening to start off with. (25) But after Brianna found me and looked after me, everything got better.

(26) Dad picked me up from school every day for my first week. (27) Then I start catch the bus. (28) The bus droped me off right out the front of my house.

(29) Now I love my new school and have many great friends. (30) I realize now how important it is to welcome them. (31) Every time new students start at Mayfield Primary School, I make sure I introduce me to them. (32) I also show them around the school and ask them to sit with me. (33) It feels great to be doing something nice for someone else. (34) Of course, Brianna is always very friendish as well and she helps me get to know the new person. (35) We are like the school's welcoming squad! (36) It's a roll I am happy to take on because I know it makes someone's difficult day a little easier.

1   Which of these shows where the comma should be placed in sentence 2?

Ⓐ   Because, we moved I had to change schools.

Ⓑ   Because we moved, I had to change schools.

Ⓒ   Because we moved I had, to change schools.

Ⓓ   Because we moved I had to change, schools.

2   In sentence 3, Deena wants to replace "very afraid" with one word with the same meaning. Which word would Deena be best to use?

Ⓐ   angry

Ⓑ   puzzled

Ⓒ   terrified

Ⓓ   thrilled

3   In sentence 6, what is the correct way to spell *scarey*?

Ⓐ   scary

Ⓑ   scarry

Ⓒ   scarrey

Ⓓ   scarrie

4   In sentence 8, which word should replace *showed*?

Ⓐ   show

Ⓑ   shows

Ⓒ   shown

Ⓓ   showing

5   In sentence 13, "have to start" is not the correct tense. Which of these uses the correct tense in the sentence?

Ⓐ   I also had to start learning new things and catching up on some work that I missed.

Ⓑ   I also will have had to start learning new things and catching up on some work that I missed.

Ⓒ   I also had been having to start learning new things and catching up on some work that I missed.

Ⓓ   I also would have been having to start learning new things and catching up on some work that I missed.

6   Which of these corrects an error at the end of sentence 15?

Ⓐ   She was very kind and gave me lots of help.

Ⓑ   She was very kind and gave me lot's of help.

Ⓒ   She was very kind and gave me lots of helps.

Ⓓ   She was very kind and gave me lot's of helps.

7   In sentence 16, the words *sure* and *wear* are both homophones. Which sentence uses the correct form of both homophones?

    Ⓐ   At lunchtime, I wasn't shore wear to sit.

    Ⓑ   At lunchtime, I wasn't shore where to sit.

    Ⓒ   At lunchtime, I wasn't sure where to sit.

    Ⓓ   At lunchtime, I wasn't sure we're to sit.

8   In sentence 17, which word should replace *so*?

    Ⓐ   but

    Ⓑ   for

    Ⓒ   or

    Ⓓ   yet

9   In sentence 19, which word should replace *tell*?

    Ⓐ   tells

    Ⓑ   told

    Ⓒ   telled

    Ⓓ   telling

10   Sentence 21 can be rewritten to express the ideas in a simpler way. Which of these is the best way to rewrite sentence 21?

Ⓐ   We also played some fun games at lunch.

Ⓑ   We also played some games, fun, at lunch.

Ⓒ   We also played some games at lunch, was fun.

Ⓓ   We also played some games at lunch, which was fun.

11   In sentence 23, the word *is* is not the correct word. Which of these writes the sentence with the correct word?

Ⓐ   He asked me how my day are.

Ⓑ   He asked me how my day was.

Ⓒ   He asked me how my day were.

Ⓓ   He asked me how my day gone.

12   In sentence 24, which word should replace *he*?

Ⓐ   his

Ⓑ   him

Ⓒ   it

Ⓓ   them

13   Which of these shows the correct way to write sentence 27?

Ⓐ   Then I started catch the bus.

Ⓑ   Then I start catching the bus.

Ⓒ   Then I started catching the bus.

Ⓓ   Then I starting catching the bus.

14   Which change should be made in sentence 28?

Ⓐ   Change *droped* to *dropped*

Ⓑ   Change *right* to *write*

Ⓒ   Change *front* to *frunt*

Ⓓ   Change *my* to *me*

15   The meaning of sentence 30 is unclear. Which words should replace *them* to make the meaning clearer?

Ⓐ   our parents

Ⓑ   old friends

Ⓒ   my teachers

Ⓓ   new students

16   Which word should replace *me* in sentence 31?

Ⓐ   myself

Ⓑ   ourself

Ⓒ   herself

Ⓓ   themself

17   In sentence 34, *friendish* is not the correct word. Which of these is the correct word to use?

Ⓐ   friendlier

Ⓑ   friendly

Ⓒ   friendless

Ⓓ   friendship

18   Which change should be made in sentence 36?

Ⓐ   Change *roll* to *role*

Ⓑ   Change *am* to *are*

Ⓒ   Change *take* to *took*

Ⓓ   Change *easier* to *easiness*

END OF PRACTICE SET

Passage 16

Sarah was asked by her English teacher to write an article about something helpful. She wrote the following article on how to care for a new pet puppy. Read the article and look for any changes that should be made. Then answer the questions that follow.

How to Care for Your New Pet Puppy

(1) Once you have bringed your new puppy home, there is a lot to do. (2) If you do these things, your puppy will be happy and you will be happy too.

(3) You need to prepare your house for the puppy. (4) You dont want it to get hurt or break anything. (5) Put away any breakable items. (6) Put away any dangerous chemicals or cleaning products. (7) Also, a trash can that is tall would be a good idea. (8) This will prevent your puppy from nocking it over and making a terrible mess.

(9) Your puppy will need a bed. (10) Prepare a bed that is dry soft and warm. (11) Give your new puppy a blanket to snuggle under. (12) At night, it might be good to make a puppy house near your bed. (13) If it is near your bed, you can hear it get up when it wants to go to the toilet.

(14) Your puppy will need a good supply of food and water. (15) Buy two bowls one will be for food and the other for water. (16) Remember to buy nutritious food for your puppy. (17) If you need help selecting the right food, talk to your vet or your parents. (18) Don't forget about treats too. (19) Treats help with training and may also be good for their teeth.

(20) Puppies also loves toys to play with. (21) It gives them something to chew on. (22) Buy a range of toys and make sure you play with your puppy offen.

(23) Regularly bath your puppy. (24) Bathing your puppy can help prevent fleas and other health problems. (25) You may also like to buy some puppy care tools such as a brush and nail clippers.

(26) Always remember to comfort your puppy by patting it gently. (27) This will help you to bond with your puppy and it feel very loved. (28) Also, because they are little and fragile and can be hurt easy, remember to handle your puppy with care.

(29) Remember to walk your puppy every day. (30) Buy a harness and a lead as soon as you can and start by walking your puppy around the house. (31) Then walk it around the block and then the neighborhood. (32) Puppies love to roam and it is also good for there health.

(33) However, it is also important to be careful when you are out and about with your puppy. (34) You should keep it on the lead at all times. (35) You might think it is safe. (36) Puppies can become curious and run off. (37) You also want to keep your puppy safe from other more large dogs.

1   In sentence 1, which word should be used in place of *bringed*?

ⓐ   bring

ⓑ   bought

ⓒ   brought

ⓓ   bringing

2   Sentence 2 can be rewritten to express the ideas in a simpler way. Which of these shows the best way to rewrite sentence 2 without changing its meaning?

ⓐ   If you do these things, you both will be happy with your puppy.

ⓑ   If you do these things, your puppy and you will both be happy.

ⓒ   If you do these things, your puppy will be happy with you too.

ⓓ   If you do these things, you and your puppy will be happy too.

3   Which of these shows where an apostrophe should be placed in sentence 4?

ⓐ   You do'nt want it to get hurt or break anything.

ⓑ   You don't want it to get hurt or break anything.

ⓒ   You dont wa'nt it to get hurt or break anything.

ⓓ   You dont wan't it to get hurt or break anything.

4   Which of these shows the best way to rewrite sentence 7 in a simpler way?

Ⓐ   Also, a tall trash can would be a good idea.

Ⓑ   Also, a trash tall can would be a good idea.

Ⓒ   Also, a trash can, tall, would be a good idea.

Ⓓ   Also, a trash can would be a good idea, tall.

5   Sentence 8 contains a spelling error. Which change should be made to correct the error?

Ⓐ   Replace *prevent* with *prevvent*

Ⓑ   Replace *nocking* with *knocking*

Ⓒ   Replace *making* with *makeing*

Ⓓ   Replace *terrible* with *terribal*

6   Which of these shows where commas should be placed in sentence 10?

Ⓐ   Prepare a bed that is, dry soft and warm.

Ⓑ   Prepare a bed that is, dry, soft, and warm.

Ⓒ   Prepare a bed that is dry, soft, and warm.

Ⓓ   Prepare a bed that is dry, soft, and, warm.

7   Which of these shows the correct way to punctuate sentence 15?

Ⓐ   Buy two bowls, one will be for food and the other for water.

Ⓑ   Buy two bowls; one will be for food and the other for water.

Ⓒ   Buy two bowls: one will be for food and the other for water.

Ⓓ   Buy two bowls! one will be for food and the other for water.

8   Which of these is the best way to rewrite sentence 18?

Ⓐ   Don't forget about treats either.

Ⓑ   Don't forget about treats neither.

Ⓒ   Don't forget about treats anything.

Ⓓ   Don't forget about treats each.

9   Which of these shows the correct way to write sentence 20?

Ⓐ   Puppies also love toys to plays with.

Ⓑ   Puppies also loves toy to play with.

Ⓒ   Puppies also love toys to play with.

Ⓓ   Puppies also loves toy to plays with.

10   Which change should be made in sentence 22?

Ⓐ   Change *toys* to *toy's*

Ⓑ   Change *make* to *made*

Ⓒ   Change *your* to *you're*

Ⓓ   Change *offen* to *often*

11   Sarah wants to rewrite the start of sentence 25 so that the sentence tells people to do something instead of suggesting people do something. Which of these shows the best way to rewrite the sentence?

Ⓐ   You could also buy some puppy care tools such as a brush and nail clippers.

Ⓑ   You might also buy some puppy care tools such as a brush and nail clippers.

Ⓒ   You should also buy some puppy care tools such as a brush and nail clippers.

Ⓓ   You mustn't also buy some puppy care tools such as a brush and nail clippers.

12   Sentence 27 needs a word added before *feel*. Which of these shows the sentence with the correct word added?

Ⓐ   This will help you to bond with your puppy and it did feel very loved.

Ⓑ   This will help you to bond with your puppy and it does feel very loved.

Ⓒ   This will help you to bond with your puppy and it will feel very loved.

Ⓓ   This will help you to bond with your puppy and it would feel very loved.

13   In sentence 28, which word should replace *easy*?

    Ⓐ   easier

    Ⓑ   easily

    Ⓒ   easiness

    Ⓓ   easiest

14   Sarah wants to add a topic sentence to the start of paragraph 8. Which sentence would Sarah be best to add before sentence 29?

    Ⓐ   Being outside with your puppy is a lot of fun.

    Ⓑ   It is important that your puppy gets enough exercise.

    Ⓒ   Keep your puppy safe by keeping it on a lead.

    Ⓓ   Puppies that are bored may start to bark.

15   In sentence 32, which word should replace *there*?

    Ⓐ   they

    Ⓑ   their

    Ⓒ   they're

    Ⓓ   the

16   Sarah wants to add the sentence below to the last paragraph.

You could lose your puppy or it could even run onto the road.

Where is the best place to add the sentence?

Ⓐ   After sentence 33

Ⓑ   After sentence 34

Ⓒ   After sentence 35

Ⓓ   After sentence 36

17   Which of these is the best way to combine sentences 35 and 36?

Ⓐ   You might think it is safe, and puppies can become curious and run off.

Ⓑ   You might think it is safe, so puppies can become curious and run off.

Ⓒ   You might think it is safe, but puppies can become curious and run off.

Ⓓ   You might think it is safe, for puppies can become curious and run off.

18   In sentence 37, which word should replace "more large"?

Ⓐ   larger

Ⓑ   largest

Ⓒ   largely

Ⓓ   largeness

END OF PRACTICE SET

Passage 17

David was concerned that the students at his school were not getting enough sleep. He wrote the following persuasive letter to the school newspaper about this issue. He hoped his letter would be published in the next edition. Read the letter and look for any changes that should be made. Then answer the questions that follow.

Letter to the School Newspaper

To the editor,

(1) I am writing to inform you about an issue in our school. (2) I have noticed that many students are coming to school tired. (3) I be worried about this because I think it will affect their happiness and learning. (4) I wish to outline the benefits of getting enough sleep. (5) Please put this information in your next edition of the *School Express*.

(6) When you sleep, you are preparing you're brain four the next day. (7) If you get enough sleep, you will be able to concentrate better and easy remember information. (8) Studies have shown that a good night's sleep improves learning and creativity.

(9) You need a good night's sleep for play as well. (10) Whether you are playing an instrament or playing sport, you need to be well rested. (11) If you don't get a good night's sleep, then you will not have the energy to fully participate. (12) Also, your decision making and problem solving skills could suffer.

(13) Sleep is also important for your emotional health. (14) If you have a good night's sleep, it will be easier to control your emotions. (15) You is more likely to feel happy and enjoy the day. (16) If you are happy, you get along with everybody. (17) You will feel motivated to be a good person and helps others.

(18) Sleep allows your body to heel and can reduce the risk of certain diseases. (19) If you are sick, sleep helps you to recover more quick. (20) It helps keep everything in your body in perfect balance. (21) Also if you sleep well you will be alert and react faster. (22) This will help to prevent poor decisions. (23) Poor decisions can put you and others at risk.

(24) I have noticed that many students are not getting enough sleep. (25) I believe that one of the problems is that technology gets in the way. (26) Many students watch television at night or use tablets or computers late at night. (27) It is easy to get carried away and lose track of time. (28) You've been watching shows or playing games for hours. (29) It can be hard to wind down and relax from this screen time. (30) People with mobile phones might also be texting with friends all evening. (31) Where is the quiet time you need to prepare yourself for sleep. (32) If you want good sleep, you need to start preparing for it early in the evening. (33) Please try to turn off the television, put down your phone, and go to bed earlier.

(34) If you get more sleep, you will learn better, play better, feel happier, and protect oneself and others. (35) These is good reasons to get more sleep.

Yours sincerely

David Monroe

Students who get enough sleep will be able to concentrate better in class.

1   In sentence 1, what is the correct way to spell *writeing*?

    Ⓐ   writing

    Ⓑ   writting

    Ⓒ   riteing

    Ⓓ   riting

2   In sentence 3, which word should replace *be*?

    Ⓐ   am

    Ⓑ   is

    Ⓒ   are

    Ⓓ   was

3   In sentence 6, the words *you're* and *four* are both homophones. Which sentence uses the correct form of both homophones?

    Ⓐ   When you sleep, you are preparing your brain four the next day.

    Ⓑ   When you sleep, you are preparing you're brain for the next day.

    Ⓒ   When you sleep, you are preparing your brain for the next day.

    Ⓓ   When you sleep, you are preparing you're brain fore the next day.

4   In sentence 7, which word should be used in place of *easy*?

Ⓐ   easily

Ⓑ   easiness

Ⓒ   easiest

Ⓓ   easier

5   In sentence 10, what is the correct way to spell *instrament*?

Ⓐ   instrument

Ⓑ   instrement

Ⓒ   instroment

Ⓓ   instriment

6   David wants to replace the word *could* in sentence 12 with a word with the same meaning. Which of these shows a way to rewrite the sentence without changing its meaning?

Ⓐ   Also, your decision making and problem solving skills may suffer.

Ⓑ   Also, your decision making and problem solving skills will suffer.

Ⓒ   Also, your decision making and problem solving skills should suffer.

Ⓓ   Also, your decision making and problem solving skills won't suffer.

7 In sentence 15, the word *is* needs to be replaced with a correct word. Which of these shows the correct replacement?

Ⓐ   You am more likely to feel happy and enjoy the day.

Ⓑ   You be more likely to feel happy and enjoy the day.

Ⓒ   You are more likely to feel happy and enjoy the day.

Ⓓ   You were more likely to feel happy and enjoy the day.

8 In sentence 17, which word should replace *helps*?

Ⓐ   help

Ⓑ   helped

Ⓒ   helping

Ⓓ   helper

9 Which change should be made in sentence 18?

Ⓐ   Replace *allows* with *allow*

Ⓑ   Replace *heel* with *heal*

Ⓒ   Replace *reduce* with *reduse*

Ⓓ   Replace *certain* with *sertain*

10   In sentence 19, the word *quick* is not the right word to use. Which of these shows the correct way to write sentence 19?

Ⓐ   If you are sick, sleep helps you to recover more quicker.

Ⓑ   If you are sick, sleep helps you to recover more quickly.

Ⓒ   If you are sick, sleep helps you to recover more quicken.

Ⓓ   If you are sick, sleep helps you to recover more quickest.

11   David wants to add a sentence before sentence 18 to introduce the ideas in the paragraph. Which sentence would David be best to add?

Ⓐ   People need more sleep than usual when they are ill.

Ⓑ   Sleep is also important for your health and safety.

Ⓒ   Many people stay up too late at night.

Ⓓ   You should make sure you sleep long enough every single night.

12   Which of these shows where commas should be placed in sentence 21?

Ⓐ   Also, if you sleep well, you will be alert and react faster.

Ⓑ   Also, if you sleep well you will be alert, and react faster.

Ⓒ   Also if you sleep well, you will be alert, and react faster.

Ⓓ   Also if you sleep well, you will be, alert and react faster.

13   In sentence 27, what does the phrase "lose track of" mean?

    Ⓐ   get confused

    Ⓑ   worry about

    Ⓒ   become rushed

    Ⓓ   forget about

14   David wants to add a transition phrase to better connect the ideas in sentences 27 and 28. Which of these shows the transition phrase that should be added to the start of sentence 28?

    Ⓐ   In the long run, you've been watching shows or playing games for hours.

    Ⓑ   Slowly but surely, you've been watching shows or playing games for hours.

    Ⓒ   Before you know it, you've been watching shows or playing games for hours.

    Ⓓ   Now and then, you've been watching shows or playing games for hours.

15   Which sentence in paragraph 6 should end with a question mark?

    Ⓐ   Sentence 30

    Ⓑ   Sentence 31

    Ⓒ   Sentence 32

    Ⓓ   Sentence 33

16   In sentence 34, which word should replace *oneself*?

Ⓐ   myself

Ⓑ   yourself

Ⓒ   herself

Ⓓ   himself

17   Which of these is the correct way to write sentence 35?

Ⓐ   These is good reason to get more sleep.

Ⓑ   These be good reason to get more sleep.

Ⓒ   These are good reasons to get more sleep.

Ⓓ   These were good reasons to get more sleep.

18   Which of these uses the correct punctuation for the closing of the letter?

Ⓐ   Yours sincerely.

Ⓑ   Yours sincerely,

Ⓒ   Yours sincerely:

Ⓓ   Yours sincerely?

END OF PRACTICE SET

Passage 18

Elias's class was asked to write a fictional story about a snowy day. Elias wrote a story about a special snowman. Read the story and look for any changes that should be made. Then answer the questions that follow.

Flurry's Great Adventure

(1) One snowy winter, Flurry the snowman was made in the middle of a large park. (2) Flurry loved watching the childs play in the snow, but at night he would get lonely. (3) One friday night, Flurry decided to venture out of the park and see the world! (4) He knew that people would be frightened if they saw a living snowman, but he also knew that most people would be sleep if he left at midnight.

(5) The first thing Flurry did was visit the river. (6) The river was at the edge of the park and he hear it flowing every night. (7) When Flurry got to the river, he dipped his hat in collected fresh water. (8) Flurry took a gulp of water and loved the taste. (9) Then, he hopped over the river and headed towards town.

(10) In town, Flurry found lots of trash on the ground. (11) Even though he was sad to see litter, he was excited to find shiny gum wrappers near his feet. (12) Flurry took the gum wrappers and made them into a shiny bracelet to where. (13) As he walked on, he admired his shiny bracelet. (14) He was sad he couldn't show anyone his creation. (15) That's when he met Blizzard!

(16) Blizzard was another snowman built in the town center. (17) Flurry was so very excited to meet a fellow snowman. (18) Blizzard loved Flurrys new bracelet so Flurry taught his new friend how to make one of his own.

(19) Together, Flurry and Blizzard found a close playground. (20) Both snowmen had a grate time going down the slides and pushing each other on the swings. (21) All his life, Flurry had wanted to play on a playground and tonight his wish was coming true! (22) Flurry and Blizzard told jokes and made up stories. (23) They laughed together all night!

(24) The two snowmen had to duck into an alley to avoid a snowplow going down the road. (25) They were scared of getting swept up by the plows. (26) There is not nothing scarier to a snowman than a snowplow! (27) Once the truck had past, they decided to lay down in the snowbanks and watch the stars.

(28) At the end of the night, Blizzard and Flurry said goodbye. (29) Let's meet again tomorrow, Blizzard suggested. (30) Flurry quickly agreed. (31) Flurry was so excited to have seen the town. (32) Couldn't wait to meet up with Blizzard again. (33) He was looking forward to more adventures.

1   Which change should be made in sentence 2?

Ⓐ   Replace *loved* with *love*

Ⓑ   Replace *childs* with *children*

Ⓒ   Replace *but* with *so*

Ⓓ   Replace *get* with *gotten*

2   Which word in sentence 3 should start with a capital letter?

Ⓐ   friday

Ⓑ   night

Ⓒ   venture

Ⓓ   world

3   In sentence 4, which word should be used in place of *sleep*?

Ⓐ   sleeps

Ⓑ   slept

Ⓒ   asleep

Ⓓ   sleeper

4   In sentence 6, which word should replace *hear*?

    Ⓐ   hears

    Ⓑ   heard

    Ⓒ   hearing

    Ⓓ   heared

5   Sentence 7 is written incorrectly. Which word should be added before *collected* to complete the sentence?

    Ⓐ   to

    Ⓑ   some

    Ⓒ   and

    Ⓓ   then

6   Elias wants to add the words *big* and *great* to sentence 8 to describe the gulp that Flurry took. Which of these shows the best placement of the words?

    Ⓐ   Flurry took a big great gulp of water and loved the taste.

    Ⓑ   Flurry took a great big gulp of water and loved the taste.

    Ⓒ   Flurry took a gulp of big great water and loved the taste.

    Ⓓ   Flurry took a gulp of great big water and loved the taste.

7   Which word could replace "Even though" at the start of sentence 11?

    Ⓐ   Yes

    Ⓑ   Sure

    Ⓒ   Then

    Ⓓ   While

8   In sentence 12, which word should replace *where*?

    Ⓐ   were

    Ⓑ   wear

    Ⓒ   we're

    Ⓓ   wore

9   In sentence 15, what is *That's* short for?

    Ⓐ   That is

    Ⓑ   That us

    Ⓒ   That goes

    Ⓓ   That does

10   In sentence 17, Elias wants to replace the words "so very excited" with one word with the same meaning. Which word would Elias be best to use?

Ⓐ   amazed

Ⓑ   surprised

Ⓒ   scared

Ⓓ   thrilled

11   Which change should be made in sentence 18?

Ⓐ   Replace *Flurrys* with *Flurry's*

Ⓑ   Replace *so* with *then*

Ⓒ   Replace *taught* with *teach*

Ⓓ   Replace *make* with *made*

12   In sentence 19, the word *close* can be replaced with a better word. Which word should replace *close*?

Ⓐ   near

Ⓑ   nearby

Ⓒ   nearly

Ⓓ   nearest

13 Which change should be made in sentence 20?

Ⓐ   Replace *had* with *have*

Ⓑ   Replace *grate* with *great*

Ⓒ   Replace *going* with *went*

Ⓓ   Replace *other* with *another*

14 Elias wants to add a word before *duck* in sentence 24 to show how the two snowmen had to move quickly to avoid the snowplow. Which of these shows the best word to add?

Ⓐ   The two snowmen had to swiftly duck into an alley to avoid a snowplow going down the road.

Ⓑ   The two snowmen had to silently duck into an alley to avoid a snowplow going down the road.

Ⓒ   The two snowmen had to shakily duck into an alley to avoid a snowplow going down the road.

Ⓓ   The two snowmen had to sweetly duck into an alley to avoid a snowplow going down the road.

15 Which of these shows the correct way to write sentence 26?

Ⓐ   There is nothing scarier to a snowman than a snowplow!

Ⓑ   There is anything scarier to a snowman than a snowplow!

Ⓒ   There is yet nothing scarier to a snowman than a snowplow!

Ⓓ   There is more anything scarier to a snowman than a snowplow!

16   Which change should be made in sentence 27?

ⓐ   Replace *past* with *passed*

ⓑ   Replace *decided* with *decide*

ⓒ   Replace *watch* with *watching*

ⓓ   Replace *stars* with *star's*

17   Which of these shows the correct way to punctuate sentence 29?

ⓐ   "Let's meet again tomorrow", Blizzard suggested.

ⓑ   "Let's meet again tomorrow," Blizzard suggested.

ⓒ   "Let's meet again tomorrow", Blizzard suggested."

ⓓ   "Let's meet again tomorrow," Blizzard suggested."

18   Which sentence from the last paragraph is NOT a complete sentence?

ⓐ   Sentence 30

ⓑ   Sentence 31

ⓒ   Sentence 32

ⓓ   Sentence 33

END OF PRACTICE SET

ANSWER KEY

Passage 1

1.B	7.A	13.B
2.A	8.B	14.B
3.A	9.C	15.B
4.A	10.D	16.D
5.C	11.A	17.B
6.D	12.A	18.B

Passage 2

1.C	7.D	13.C
2.C	8.B	14.A
3.C	9.D	15.B
4.B	10.A	16.C
5.A	11.B	17.A
6.C	12.B	18.C

Passage 3

1.B	7.A	13.A
2.D	8.C	14.D
3.A	9.B	15.B
4.C	10.C	16.C
5.C	11.A	17.C
6.B	12.A	18.C

Passage 4

1.B	7.C	13.D
2.C	8.B	14.D
3.A	9.C	15.D
4.A	10.B	16.A
5.A	11.B	17.A
6.B	12.C	18.C

Passage 5

1.D	7.D	13.D
2.A	8.C	14.C
3.C	9.B	15.B
4.C	10.D	16.A
5.B	11.A	17.B
6.A	12.C	18.C

Passage 6

1.B	7.C	13.B
2.A	8.B	14.B
3.B	9.A	15.C
4.A	10.C	16.A
5.B	11.A	17.D
6.D	12.A	18.C

Passage 7

1.A	7.D	13.C
2.C	8.B	14.A
3.C	9.D	15.C
4.A	10.A	16.C
5.B	11.C	17.A
6.C	12.C	18.B

Passage 8

1.C	7.B	13.B
2.D	8.C	14.B
3.A	9.D	15.A
4.B	10.B	16.B
5.B	11.C	17.A
6.A	12.B	18.B

Passage 9

1.C	7.A	13.B
2.C	8.A	14.B
3.A	9.B	15.D
4.C	10.B	16.A
5.B	11.A	17.C
6.B	12.C	18.D

Passage 10

1.A	7.C	13.A
2.A	8.A	14.C
3.C	9.A	15.C
4.B	10.B	16.D
5.D	11.B	17.C
6.C	12.A	18.B

Passage 11

1.C	7.A	13.A
2.A	8.C	14.C
3.B	9.A	15.C
4.B	10.C	16.B
5.A	11.A	17.C
6.A	12.D	18.A

Passage 12

1.D	7.C	13.B
2.B	8.A	14.C
3.D	9.D	15.D
4.A	10.A	16.C
5.D	11.C	17.D
6.C	12.A	18.B

Passage 13

1.D	7.A	13.B
2.C	8.D	14.C
3.A	9.A	15.A
4.A	10.D	16.A
5.B	11.B	17.D
6.C	12.D	18.A

Passage 14

1.B	7.C	13.C
2.B	8.A	14.A
3.B	9.B	15.B
4.A	10.B	16.B
5.A	11.A	17.A
6.C	12.D	18.A

Passage 15

1.B	7.C	13.C
2.C	8.A	14.A
3.A	9.B	15.D
4.C	10.A	16.A
5.A	11.B	17.B
6.A	12.B	18.A

Passage 16

1.C	7.B	13.B
2.B	8.A	14.B
3.B	9.C	15.B
4.A	10.D	16.D
5.B	11.C	17.C
6.C	12.C	18.A

Passage 17

1.A	7.C	13.D
2.A	8.A	14.C
3.C	9.B	15.B
4.A	10.B	16.B
5.A	11.B	17.C
6.A	12.A	18.B

Passage 18

1.B	7.D	13.B
2.A	8.B	14.A
3.C	9.A	15.A
4.B	10.D	16.A
5.C	11.A	17.B
6.B	12.B	18.C

Made in the USA
San Bernardino, CA
26 February 2019